The Library Student
Advisory Board

The Library Student Advisory Board

Why Your Academic Library Needs It and How to Make It Work

Amy L. Deuink *and*
Marianne Seiler

McFarland & Company, Inc., Publishers
Jefferson, North Carolina, and London

LIBRARY OF CONGRESS CATALOGUING-IN-PUBLICATION DATA

Deuink, Amy.
The library student advisory board : why your academic library needs
it and how to make it work / Amy L. Deuink and Marianne Seiler.
p.   cm.
Includes bibliographical references and index.

ISBN 978-0-7864-3560-9
softcover : 50# alkaline paper ∞

1. Academic libraries — Administration.   2. Penn State
Schuylkill. Library Student Advisory Board.   3. Ciletti Memorial
Library — Administration.   4. Library clubs.   5. Libraries and colleges.
I. Seiler, Marianne, 1960–   II. Title.
Z675.U5D48   2009   025.1'977 — dc22   2008044276

British Library cataloguing data are available

Cover images ©2009 Shutterstock.

Manufactured in the United States of America

McFarland & Company, Inc., Publishers
Box 611, Jefferson, North Carolina 28640
www.mcfarlandpub.com

268952968

To all our past, present and future LSAB members.
Many thanks for your hard work and dedication.

Acknowledgments

"If I have seen further it is by standing on the shoulders of Giants."— Isaac Newton

My achievements would not be possible without the giants in my life. Thank you to family and friends who have helped me through the writing of this book. Thinking of all the strong women I know has given me the strength to carry on during the hard times.

To Marianne, I am grateful for your vision and enthusiasm for the club, your encouragement while writing this book together, and your friendship forever.

Amy L. Deuink

First I would like to thank my husband Rick and my children, Erika and Jonathan, for supporting me in everything I do.

Thanks to Rosanne Chesakis for all the grammar and editing help over the years and Vince Mitchell for helping me edit all the pictures for this book.

A special thanks to my mom, Phyllis Ann Snyder, who passed away during the writing of this book. Mom, you were my biggest fan.

Thanks to all the LSAB members who have been there for me and thanks to our Campus Librarian, Mr. Michael W. Loder, and the library staff, Susan Martin, Rosanne Chesakis and Vince Mitchell, for all their support.

To Amy, my best friend, this wouldn't be possible without you. You're the greatest!

Marianne Seiler

Thank you to every member — past and present — of the Library Student Advisory Board at Penn State Schuylkill. This book would not have been possible without your interest, your ideas, or your hard work. Special thanks to Rosanne Chesakis, Ashley Fehr, Nick Freer, Anthony Phillips, Loni Picarella, Hannah Tracy, and Patrick Troutman for their contributions to this book.

Table of Contents

Table of Contents

Preface

This book is a practical guide for people wishing to establish an active library student advisory group at their own campus, based on five years of real-world experience. In fact, anyone wishing to start an active student club of any kind will find this book useful. We define a library student advisory board as a group of students working with their campus library to help make the library more student-centered and to bring more students to the library. Our Library Student Advisory Board (LSAB) is different from traditional academic library friends groups or models for students advising the library. The LSAB is composed entirely of students and is a university sanctioned student club receiving university funding. Students give us feedback, but also promote the library to their peers and raise funds for donations of materials of *student* choice. The activities of the club not only benefit the library — they benefit the entire campus community and the local community around it.

Marianne was the big advocate of a library club at our campus and was very excited to receive the green light to get the club started and be appointed the de facto club advisor. She was so excited that she took off like a shot, not really thinking about what steps she should take to create an organization that would be successful. But with determination, some good advice, and a lot of hard work, the Library Student Advisory Board has become a thriving club on campus — and we had a tremendous amount of fun in the process. We hope you can use this book to have the same success with a library student advisory board of your own.

In this book you will find advice on how to get your club started, recruit new members, and keep your members active, as well as material on duties of the club advisor, do's and don'ts of fund-raising, and building the club's relationship with library directors and staff.

You may be asking yourself, "Why would we want to start a library club?" Well, here are a few reasons:

- Students want to volunteer their time to serve their community and make the library a better place, so take advantage of this!
- Realize increased library usage due to club efforts. Once the club gets students in the library, though, it is the library's job to show them what it has to offer them. You are the experts on this.

- Receive advice on ways to make the library more student-centered and appealing to your target audience.
- Student involvement on campus promotes student retention.
- The club is an opportunity to build unexpected long-lasting friendships with students, faculty, and staff in other departments.
- Finally, you will have fun doing it!

Chapter 1 explains why we started our Library Student Advisory Board and elaborates upon the reasons why you should consider starting a library student advisory board at your library. It also explains the unique circumstances of our small campus and the community in which it resides, and demystifies the complexity of the large university system to which we belong. We find that there are both benefits and disadvantages to belonging to a large university system. Also in this chapter, library staff member Rosanne Chesakis paints a vivid portrait of the library at the Penn State Schuylkill campus and reflects on the importance of the LSAB to our library.

Chapter 2 tells the story of how our club got started, including Marianne's creative recruitment techniques, and briefly shows how the club has benefited our library, our campus, and our community. Throughout this chapter we also start to point out the things you will need to do to start a club of your own. This chapter also contains three student reflections on club membership from past club leaders.

Chapter 3 details the qualities of a good club advisor and what we believe to be the typical responsibilities of a person in this position. This chapter will help readers determine who at their library is the best candidate for the job, and help the individual appointed as advisor to understand what the position entails. As long as the advisor can commit a little bit of time to helping the club achieve its goals, we believe that anyone ready for the job can make their club a success.

We hope that by the time the reader reaches chapter 4 he or she will have decided that a library student advisory board is right for his or her library, and now is ready to begin working on getting a library club started. This chapter offers tips on getting your club started and conducting its first meetings, based on our experience. It also contains two more student reflections. The first shares a student's thoughts on making the library a welcome place for everyone, providing a good deal of insight into how undergraduates view our libraries. The second shows a student's excitement at finding such a club on campus and includes a reflection on club meetings.

Chapters 5–7 build on the responsibilities of the club advisor, as described in chapter 3. Chapter 5 discusses the importance of understanding and helping your students interpret policies and procedures at your college or university. Since these will be unique to each school, we suggest important policies to learn about for your club. This chapter also discusses the importance of keeping good records and demonstrates why record keeping is crucial. Chapter 6 shares our club's specific goals and objectives, and offers suggestions for developing your own. Most of the chapter, however, discusses ways to meet these goals. We also offer tips on building relationships with your club members, keeping both them and yourself motivated, and discovering students' needs and desires — essential elements for achieving your goals. Chapter 7 discusses the importance of promoting your club on campus and continually recruiting new members.

Chapter 8 goes into detail about the achievements of our club, offering ideas for readers to use with their own clubs. The chapter is broken down into three segments: activities contributing to the library, activities contributing to the campus, and activities contributing to the community.

Chapter 9 offers tips for helping the club work with the library and the campus to achieve its goals. Often, as someone who can understand both sides, it may be the job of the advisor to act as an interpreter between the club and library or campus administration. In another student reflection, a former club leader recalls her own experience forging a relationship with the new campus chancellor. This chapter concludes with examples of how Amy, as a reference and instruction librarian, benefited from working with the club.

In chapter 10 we end with an exploration of the directions our Library Student Advisory Board could possibly take in the future, in light of the directions it is currently headed. Our ideas for the future may be ideas readers would wish to use to get their own club started.

Still not convinced? In the Epilogue we explore possible reasons for hesitation and revisit some ideas, techniques, and tips readers could use to break down any roadblocks that might be preventing them from taking those first steps toward starting a library student advisory board at their campus.

We encourage readers considering starting their own library club — or any campus club — to read through the chapters sequentially. Library administrators and library staff may play different roles with their library student advisory board, and we think this book will be equally informative for both. However, as this book is written to be a practical guide, it is written with the club advisor in mind. Chapter 2 offers information on getting a club started and holding its first meetings. Chapters 3–7 and 9 primarily detail the role and responsibilities of the advisor, making it easy for users to flip to a particular section in these chapters for tips. And chapters 8 and 10 can be used to generate ideas for club activities, especially when a club is just getting started.

1

Introduction

This book is a practical guide for people wishing to establish an active library student advisory group at their own campus, based on real-world experience. In fact, this book could help anyone interested in helping students plan, establish, and develop an active campus club of any kind. In this book you will discover how to get a club like this started, and also read about the benefits we have reaped at Penn State Schuylkill. Different from traditional models of students advising the library or academic library friends groups, our club is comprised of volunteers from our target population. Students give us advice, but also promote the library to their peers and raise funds for donations of materials of *student* choice.

In this book you will read about why and how we started our Library Student Advisory Board in order to help you decide if a club such as this is right for your library. If you are ready to start a group of your own, we will offer guidance for establishing a university-sanctioned club, conducting those tenuous first meetings, recruiting new members, and keeping your members active. We will illustrate what it takes to be a student club advisor, share our experience with managing the work involved, and offer some techniques we found helpful in keeping members motivated. Included are ideas for club activities that contribute to the library, the campus, and the community beyond the university. We will explore fund-raising, promoting your club on campus, and building a strong relationship between the library's decision-makers and student club members in order to build respect and affect change. The activities of the club not only benefit the library, they benefit the entire campus community.

Why We Started the Library Student Advisory Board

Like many college and university libraries, we at Penn State Schuylkill had been facing declining use of our circulating collections, reference services, and, unfortunately, the library as a whole during the past decade. As our collections increasingly become electronically accessible, it seems students may find less need to come in to

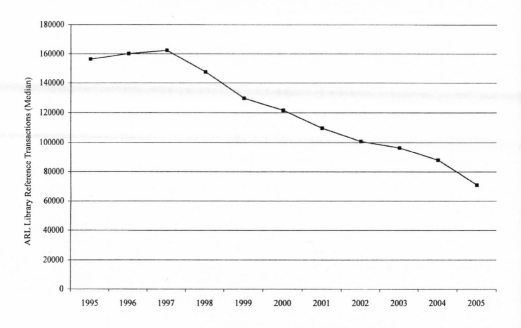

Association of Research Libraries (ARL) library reference transactions, 1995–2005.

the library. And perhaps an increase in information literacy instruction over the past decade has helped more students help themselves, explaining the decline in reference transactions (see Graph 1).[1] The library had become quiet, yet the desire to feel needed, to feel that our services are in demand, still lingers. So we campaign to get students back into the library to discover the tools and treasures they've been missing.

Our Library Student Advisory Board (LSAB) started as a way to find out what students thought of the library so that we could combat misconceptions with targeted marketing and outreach. It was a way to get input about library collections and policies to help us appeal to students who weren't using the library. But it has turned into much more. Not only did we find that club members had a lot of ideas to help us improve students' experience when using the library, but that they could actually get excited about making the library a better place. Members also became excited about letting their peers know about what the library contains and what they have done to help improve it.

Even though the idea for this student group came from the library, it was established by students and is run by students. The club's advisor offers a voice from within the library and helps guide the trajectory of the group. The union of an independent, university-sanctioned student club with a club advisor from the library staff has, so far, proven to be the perfect marriage. Much like the friends groups often found at public libraries, we receive feedback and donations from this independent student group. In return, students see that they have a voice in the library when we act upon their suggestions. They also get to see how their fund-raising and library donations benefit the entire campus community.

About Our Library

Rosanne Chesakis, a long-time Ciletti Memorial Library staff member and Penn State alumna, paints a vivid portrait of the scene in which we work and the place where a notion for the Library Student Advisory Board at the Penn State Schuylkill campus was formed. Her 23 years of experience at Penn State Schuylkill and the campus library, ranging from her time as student to her current position as the library's circulation supervisor, shines through in her deep reflection on what the LSAB has meant for us.

Reflections on the Library Student Advisory Board
by Rosanne Chesakis

Twenty years ago, our campus library didn't have a name. It didn't have its own building. It was one room in the basement of the classroom building. It had seven rows of stacks, a small reference area, nine tables for group study and socializing, and a row of carrels for independent study. It had exposed pipes that loudly announced any plumbing activity occurring on the floor above, loud fans that attempted to keep the air moving in the summer, noisy dehumidifiers to combat the perpetual dampness of the basement, and no office space. The staff, the phones, and the office machines were out in the middle of everything. Each year our underground location assured that we would experience at least one minor flood.

But what that nameless campus library did have was a central location. The building was the busiest on campus, visited daily by most of our mainly commuter student body. The only other gathering place on campus was a cavernous, chaotic room containing vending machines, battered lunch tables, and Ping-Pong tables. So the library became a place for studying, socializing, napping, relaxing, tutoring, researching, surreptitiously eating lunch (in the days when food was not allowed in the library), and generally passing time between classes.

In 1994, at long last, our new library building opened. Two whole floors of library! Climate controlled! No flooding! Quiet plumbing! Office and meeting space! It was an attractive and welcoming space, filled with state-of-the-art resources and technologies. But it was no longer centrally located on campus. A trip to the library required extra effort and a particularly long walk from the parking lot. And the fact that the opening of our new library coincided with the Internet revolution, a widespread decline in the use of academic libraries, and an era when both faculty and students were beginning to question the library's place in the "everything is on the Internet" mindset, meant that the road ahead would not be smooth.

During the 1990s, libraries everywhere were forced to think about programming, marketing, and creative approaches to usage. Gone were the days when using the library was a given and library staff just had to "be there," assured of a ready market for their services. Our location challenges added to the dilemma, but our situation was certainly not unique.

Libraries have met and overcome these challenges in many ways, but for us, the Library Student Advisory Board was a particularly effective and enjoyable way of bringing our library into the twenty-first century. The students in the club have acted as an honest, critical sounding board for our ideas, and have generated quite a few ideas of their own. They tell us what they think will work; they brainstorm, dream, and scheme. We remind them of university regulations and fiscal constraints. Together, we arrive at solutions that are the better for the wide variety of input.

The LSAB has benefited students in ways more far-reaching than a hot lunch once a month and the availability of gaming consoles in the library. The opportunity to develop leadership skills extends to other organizations students may be involved with and enriches their college experience. Our club is well known as one which gets things done, and as a result our students are in demand to serve in other capacities on campus.

The LSAB also gives our students a sense of connectedness to the campus. The opportunity to interact with (and often develop close relationships with) faculty, staff and administrators lets the students know that their opinions are valid, enriches their campus experience, and helps to ensure that, in the midst of a large university, they will not be lost in the crowd. Students who get to feel comfortable with the library staff and faculty through the club will often come looking for a sympathetic ear, bringing their academic or personal problems to the attention of the library staff. We can direct them to the appropriate resources if needed, or just act as a sounding board to let them know they have somewhere to turn.

Club officers and members are also gaining experience useful to them as they move on into other educational settings or their careers. Many students have told us they were glad they became familiar with the library at our small campus, because it made the huge libraries they subsequently encountered on larger campuses much less intimidating. They also gain valuable skills and experience which they take with them into their careers.

Today we are still glad to have the spacious, attractive library with climate control, quiet plumbing and diversified spaces. It's still a long walk from the parking lot. But now it buzzes with students availing themselves of not just books and periodicals, but DVDs, game consoles, board games, jigsaw puzzles and vending machines. It has once again become the place to pass time socializing, studying, and enjoying the many other options it offers. The Library Student Advisory Board has been the tool to mold the library into a place more responsive to student needs and wants, and to empower the students to be involved and invested in their campus. It's been a win-win situation.

About Our Campus

Throughout this book we will often refer to "our campus" and occasionally "University Libraries." The Pennsylvania State University is "one university, geographically dispersed" and our campus, the Schuylkill Campus, is just one of twenty-four campuses across the state. We are one part of a large, complex system that has been developed over 150 years. It works for us, but some of the challenges we face might not exist at other universities. Perhaps you face different challenges. We hope you will be able to apply what we have learned from our experience to your own situation.

What is known today as the Pennsylvania State University was established in 1855 as the Farmers' High School of Pennsylvania, chartered to teach students to apply scientific principles to farming. The Farmers' High School was established at the site that is known today as the University Park Campus. In 1862 the Farmers' High School was renamed the Agricultural College of Pennsylvania. Also in 1862 Congress passed the Morrill Land Grant Act, providing for the endowment of state universities. The following year, the college was appointed as Pennsylvania's land-grant university. Starting with 119 students in 1859 (following the completion of the original college building, now "Old Main"), the university has grown to serve over 90,000 students. Approximately half of the students enrolled at the university are located at the University Park Campus and half are enrolled at other campus locations across the state, including the Dickenson School of Law, the College of Medicine, and the World Campus. Reportedly, one out of every 114 Americans with a college degree is a Penn State graduate.[2]

Many students choose to start their university education at one of the regional campuses throughout the state and finish their degree program at one of the larger campuses. The regional campuses are closer to home for many and others choose to make the transition to college in the intimate atmosphere provided by a smaller campus, where students can receive individual attention. In addition, many campuses have unique programs of study designed to serve the needs of their local communities and also offer graduate-level programs. Now one of the smallest campuses in the university system, the Schuylkill Campus enrolled 940 students in the Fall 2007 semester, with fewer than one in three (260 of 940 students) residing on campus.

When people think of Penn State, popular images such as Old Main, Creamery ice cream, Beaver Stadium, and football coach extraordinaire Joe Paterno may come to mind. In fact, we recently heard that Penn State is the only university to have a library named for the football coach and a football stadium named for a university president. (James A. Beaver was President of the Board of Trustees and served as interim President of the University from 1906 to 1908.) If we're not the only ones, there aren't many. These images all originate from the University Park campus. But in 1934 four regional campuses were chartered across the state to serve the needs of residents, many of whom could not afford to relocate to University Park in the midst of the Great Depression. Over the years, many other regional and special-mission campuses would be established.

Located in the city of Pottsville, the Pottsville Center was one of the four original regional campuses chartered in 1934. Enrollment at the university boomed following World War II and in 1967 the Pottsville Center was relocated six miles south to the borough of Schuylkill Haven and renamed the Schuylkill Campus of the Pennsylvania State University. Here the campus would have formal buildings and grounds, rather than lease buildings in the city.

Our campus is situated in the Appalachian Mountains of eastern Pennsylvania. The borough of Schuylkill Haven sits near the origin of the Little Schuylkill River, a tributary of the Schuylkill River flowing though eastern Pennsylvania into Philadelphia, then into the Delaware River, and on to the Atlantic Ocean. It is said that the term "schuylkill" (pronounced ˈskü-kʾl or ˈskül-kil according to *Merriam-Webster's Collegiate Dictionary*) is derived from the Dutch phrase "Schuilen-Kil," meaning "hidden stream."[3] This region is rich in the proud, if sometimes sordid, history of anthracite coal mining. Even today you can see remnants of the canals where a century ago barges hauled tons of anthracite coal down from the mountains to Philadelphia. Anthracite coal is valued for burning slower and hotter than bituminous coal and was used to fuel the nation's industrial revolution. Though coal mining ravaged much of the landscape, over the decades nature has reclaimed and restored much of its original beauty. Hikers along the Appalachian Trail get breathtaking views of the valleys below. The local area also boasts the homes of authors John O'Hara and Conrad Richter; the Yuengling Brewery (since 1829, America's oldest continuously operating brewery); the Molly Maguires and the 1877 "Day of the Rope"; and a National Football League (NFL) team known from 1925 to 1928 as the Pottsville Maroons. This fact would be fairly insignificant, but serious football fans out there will know that the Maroons were on the losing end of a long-disputed NFL decision for 1925 league champion. The Pottsville Maroons were denied their claim to the title as the result of a controversial call by the league president, which ultimately awarded the title to the Chicago Cardinals instead. In the hearts of locals, the Maroons will always be the true 1925 NFL champions.

Books and documents relating to local history such as this can be found in the Ciletti Memorial Library at the Schuylkill Campus. The Ciletti Library is part of the Penn State system of university libraries, providing library collections and services at all the campuses that make up the university. Like the university, the university library system can also be characterized as "one library, geographically dispersed," with the highest levels of administration centralized at the University Park campus. Books and other items are dispersed across the campuses and our students have access to all materials in the system, giving students at a small campus access to all the resources typically found in a large university research library. While some policies and practices are established system-wide, we do exercise some local control in order to meet the specific needs of our students. Being a small library on a small campus within a large system can have its disadvantages. We try to offer a large range of service hours to accommodate any student's schedule, and variety in our collections and services to meet student needs, but there will always be students who want more. However, limits to what we can do to meet student demands are defined by our staff of two professional librarians and four library support staff members. We do rely on student workers and volunteers from the club to help us in times of need. So, throughout this book you might read about students helping with projects you might not trust to a student. Sometimes we do so out of necessity, but in our experience it has proven to be a good working relationship.

Culture of Community Service

If we look at the big picture, the club can mean more than simply students advising the library in order to develop targeted marketing and outreach, or students finding a way to get entertainment they want into the library's collection. Students are coming to college having reflected on how serving their community has changed their lives and improved the lives of the community members they served. The skills students bring and improve with their involvement in the club can be carried into their professional careers and encourage civic involvement through college and beyond. Furthermore, involvement with a club such as a library student advisory board that helps integrate new students into the campus community may even contribute to students' retention at the university.

According to a recent survey of American youth, 55 percent of those aged twelve to eighteen volunteered through a formal organization in 2004.[4] By comparison, a different survey found that only 24 percent of those aged sixteen to twenty-four volunteered in that same year.[5] We suspect that the rate of volunteerism might be higher among the younger students because many school districts across America have instituted service-learning in the classroom and some schools are even making community service a high school graduation requirement. A positive indicator for the state of youth volunteerism, the survey of the younger group found that students who participated in a service-learning course that included both reflection and planning and that lasted at least one semester were 71 percent more likely than students who had *never* engaged in service-learning to volunteer in the upcoming year.[6] A total of 38 percent of students surveyed indicated current or past participation in school-based community service.[7]

Service-learning is more than just volunteering one's time to serve an organization. It is community service integrated with school curriculum, and requires involvement beyond the volunteer activity itself. The purpose is to enrich students' learning experience, teach civic responsibility, and strengthen local communities.[8] According to the Corporation for National and Community Service (CNCS), generally accepted elements of high-quality service-learning include planning the service activity, participating in regular service for a semester or longer, and writing or reflecting on the service experience.[9] Testing shows that these three elements, of the eleven essential

11

elements as defined by the National Service-Learning Cooperative, are essential in order for the service-learning to have a positive impact on students.[10] Standards for service-learning were developed by the Alliance for Service-Learning in Educational Reform in 1995[11] and later updated in 1998 by the National Service-Learning Cooperative. More information about service-learning can be found online at the National Service-Learning Clearinghouse, a program of Learn and Serve America, an initiative of the CNCS, at www.servicelearning.org.

We believe that as a result of their volunteer experience, students are coming to campus with a desire to get involved, to contribute to their new campus community — *and believe they can make a difference*. Students gain the satisfaction of improving the lives of those around them, while making new friends and gaining experiences valued in the workplace in the process. Some students also already have the experience and leadership skills that come with planning volunteer or service-learning activities and have seen the difference a sustained effort can make in their community. Some even come to college with unexpected skills, whether it is familiarity with library processes from volunteering at their local public library, sensitivity and a smile from working at a hospital or nursing home, or construction skills from working on a local building project. Don't be surprised if many students want to get involved with your group, as well as several other organizations in your campus community. And if you take the time to find out what unique skills students on your campus have and recruit students with a variety of talents to your club, you will find you have developed a well-rounded membership.

State of Volunteerism: Role of Service Learning

The CNCS is a public-private partnership that engages Americans of all ages in service through three national service initiatives: AmeriCorps, the National Senior Service Corps, and Learn and Serve America, which provides models and resources for teachers integrating service into classrooms from kindergarten through college. Recently, the CNCS conducted a series of surveys on youth volunteerism.[12] More than three-quarters (77 percent) of school-based service-learning contains one or more of the typical elements, with half (51 percent) requiring students to write or reflect on their experience and approximately one-third requiring participation in planning the activity (36 percent) and/or participation for a semester or longer (36 percent).[13]

According to the CNCS, 38 percent of today's students — approximately 10.6 million teenagers — report current or past engagement in community service as part of a school activity or requirement.[14] Furthermore, many students are helping to plan the activities or reflect and write on their service experience, indicators that students were engaged in a service-learning activity. According to the survey, of the

65 percent of students engaged in some type of school-based community service, 36 percent helped to plan their service project and 51 percent reflected on their service experience in class.[15] The CNCS found that nearly one-quarter (22 percent) of students who participated in a high-quality service program involving these elements believe that they can personally make a great deal of difference in their community, while only 8 percent of students involved in programs without these elements reported feeling the this way.[16] Students who believe that they can make a great deal of difference in their community are a great asset to a library student advisory board.

In the CNCS survey, it is interesting to note that only 5 percent of teens attribute their volunteer activities to a school requirement.[17] The CNCS found that it is parents and other family members that have the strongest influence on teen volunteerism and note that the more role models teens have, the more likely they are to volunteer.[18] The number of student volunteers grows to an impressive 15.5 million teenagers — that is a rate of 55 percent — volunteering through a formal organization, often through a religious organization or with a parent, when the activity takes place outside of school.[19] In 2005 alone, teens contributed more than 1.3 billion hours of service.

Community service and service-learning have been growing trends in America's schools over the past twenty years as educators come to recognize the value of service in the academic and professional development of today's youth.[20] In 1999 the Department of Education surveyed school principals and found that 46 percent of public high schools and 38 percent of middle schools were offering service-learning opportunities for their students and 83 percent of high school and 77 percent of middle schools were organizing volunteer opportunities without service-learning elements.[21] An independent study conducted in 2004 indicates that these numbers have stabilized over recent years, reporting that 81 percent of public high schools offer community service activities and 44 percent of public high schools offer service-learning activities.[22] However, these numbers are a drastic change from 1984, when only 9 percent of public high schools reported service-learning opportunities and 27 percent reported community service opportunities for students.[23]

How a Culture of Community Service Benefits You

Research indicates a positive correlation between civic engagement and college attendance, showing that young people with at least some college experience have higher levels of civic involvement than their peers without college experience.[24] Other research shows that the more regularly an individual volunteers, the more likely he or she is to be civically and politically engaged in other ways.[25] This is something we have observed among our students. Members of the LSAB are very likely to be involved with other organizations on campus, including the student government and other community service organizations such as Key Club. We have observed that club members involved with other organizations are more likely to take on a leadership role in the club and often make better leaders because of the diversity of their experience. The club also benefits from sharing ideas and collaborating with other clubs in creative ways. Additionally, students involved with student government, faculty senate, alumni society and other such groups on campus can exert some influence on decisions made that can benefit the club and the library. There is great potential for club members to take what they have learned from their experience with the club and apply it to leadership and volunteer opportunities in their profession and in their community after college.

The students themselves also benefit from a culture of community service. School is a place where students begin to develop their individual identities, particularly once in college and away from their home and family for the first time. And they begin to develop new identities as part of a new community — their campus community. There are many ways students build their identity — through their choice of clothing, the classes they take, or artistic expression in their corner of the dorm room that separates their space from the space of their roommates. Other ways students build identity include visible contribution to their campus community and involvement in clubs that represent their interests and values. In addition, according to the CNCS, research has shown that the results of volunteering through school can include improvements in self-esteem and academic achievement, as well as a reduction in the likelihood of involvement in the risky behaviors common on today's college campuses.[26]

A major finding from the CNCS surveys was that the strongest predictor of volunteering attitudes and behaviors among today's students is current or past participation in school-based service, followed by likelihood of voting regularly, interest in politics, belief in personal efficacy, and interest in current events.[27] This means that the most likely candidates for membership in your club — the students you should try to recruit — are the ones with past volunteering experience, and the ones who express or demonstrate an interest in voting, politics, or current events. And it will probably be easy to attract to your club any students who believe that they can make a difference in their community when you share the club's past accomplishments with them. In our experience, most of our club members have demonstrated at least one, if not many, of the above characteristics. If you do not find students with previous volunteer or service-learning experience, investigate service-learning opportunities on your own campus. Students involved in service-learning will make great club members, and faculty teaching courses with a service-learning component could become a great friend of the library student advisory board. You may even find an opportunity for a partnership here.

- DISCOVER UNIQUE SKILLS AND TALENTS

Many students come to campus with a unique set of skills from previous education, work, and volunteering experiences. Some may even possess a special talent, such as expert knowledge of a software program or a talent for entertaining as the school's costumed mascot. A talented mascot can really get the crowd excited and involved during special events at your library.

Get to know as many students as possible — particularly new students looking to find their place on campus. Find out what their passions are and where their talents lie — and take advantage of these interests. Invite students with unique skills and talents to join the club and offer their talents to the group. Not only will this help make the club relevant to members, but will also serve to keep them active and involved with the club. You find as you get to know club members better over time, new interests and talents will also surface.

The following are some examples of talents found in our students that you might look for in your own student body.

Leadership Experience. It is no surprise that students with past leadership experience (school clubs, religious organizations, etc.) typically make great leaders. You will find these students have an innate sense of the things that need to be done (budget; reports; recruitment; bargaining, haggling and/or sweet-talking to get what they want) and will draw on past experience to contribute new ideas to the club. Finding students with previous leadership experience has been important for us, since we are located at a campus with a lot of first- and second-year students and few juniors and seniors to serve as our leaders. Students leaving to finish their degree programs at larger campuses in the university system creates a lot of turnover in our group membership.

Financial Savvy. A student with an interest in banking and investments, with a shrewd flair for finance, made a great club treasurer. Somewhat uncharacteristic of his generation's spend-spend-spend attitude, this treasurer lobbied the group to thoughtfully consider each purchase and even had to be persuaded by other club members that the purchase of a small color printer for creating more attractive signs for club events was worth the cost.

Powerful and Persuasive Writing and Speaking Ability. Some students are great writers. Though the role of secretary might immediately come to mind for a student with great writing skills, this skill is also invaluable in the student serving as the club's president or vice president. This is particularly true if the student is a good persuasive writer when it comes time to request funds for the club or generate activity reports that will influence future allotments. Good writers are also often good speakers, helping them become strong leaders in the club and positive representatives of the club on campus and in their community.

Artistic Flair. Students with a talent for the visual arts have created visually engaging displays and contributed signage and other items to draw attention to these displays. Other artistic projects include posters for a variety of events. A club member with scrapbooking experience led the development of several very attractive posters highlighting the career of a former music faculty member. Students used photographs, programs, and other memorabilia from the library's campus history archive to create the posters using methods that would not damage the valuable artifacts while on display. A student with interest and experience in photography was able to use his talent — and often his own equipment — to photograph club and library events, such as the library's open house. Students with the shutter bug also revived an old library tradition of keeping a photographic record of current campus faculty. (This is a project much more manageable on a small campus than a large one.)

Dancing Shoes. Some students have natural rhythm and make great dancers. While it may not seem that knowing all the moves has much to do with the library, our club members have found a way. Club members heard that many students felt there should be more dances held on campus. Dancing is an activity many seem to enjoy, but students used to having their choice of local dance clubs do not find many options near our somewhat rural campus. In response, club members decided to sponsor a dance. Again, while this does not seem to have much to do with the library, it did promote student awareness of the club and we were able to recruit new members by being associated with the dance. Members felt the dance was so successful that the students decided to hold another, this time the dance with a Latin/salsa theme. They even brought in dance instructors to teach students some new moves before the dance. Members also created a theme-related display of films and books in the library to promote the dance and use of library materials. If student club regulations permit, this would also be a great way to raise additional funds for your club.

Movie Knowledge. Some students are movie mavens and when they find out that the club is responsible for purchasing popular DVDs for the library, you might find that you have a few new members. Some years you might even find that film buffs make up a disproportionate portion of your club. Just go with the flow. One year club members might decide that movies are their main focus, and the next year it might be video games, or graphic novels.

Other Pop Culture Savvy. We all might like to think we know what's hip, what's cool, what's happening — but frankly, it can be exhausting to keep up with all the changing trends in youth culture. Members of your club live the life. They know what their peers are interested in — it's the same thing *they* are interested in — and understanding this is part of the reason we wanted to start a club and make the library more relevant to students' needs. Some people, however, have a talent for predicting upcoming trends. And people immersed in a subculture can see changes happening within the group far sooner than an outsider will. A few years ago it was difficult to see the potential for video games in education, making it hard for students to make the case for gaming in the library. Over time, though, the relationship slowly became clearer and it was easier for students to make their case. And we probably wouldn't have ever tried holding a poetry slam until one club member took the initiative to make her vision a reality. Go with your instincts when deciding which "radical" suggestions made by your club members you can implement at your library, but remember that the suggestions are coming from an insider in the student subculture.

Technological Savvy. You will find that many students are tech-savvy (though not always as savvy as they think) and that some will display the geekish enthusiasm of a technophile. Today's students are born digital, most never knowing a life without a computer and barely remembering a time without the Internet. Their cell phone is never far away and text messaging is quickly replacing the former communication mode du jour, instant messaging. Students can help keep the library aware of popular tools and social networks that the library can use to communicate with and market themselves to the students. At the students' request, you, as advisor, might also be asked to communicate with them in other ways, such as through Facebook (www.facebook.com) or through group meeting areas offered by your university's class content management system (Blackboard, WebCT, etc.). Your technophiles can also be helpful in day-to-day troubleshooting of everyday library technology. One student working with us on a summer project noted that the sluggishness of the program we asked him to use was due to the fact that the program was commanding up to 98 percent of the laptop computer's available memory, while we had written off the sluggishness as "just the way it is." By closing unnecessary applications running in the task bar, we were able to slightly improve the performance of the software and speed up the pace of the project.

Bibliophilism. Other students just like to read. Really! We know that today's students have a reputation for possessing short attention spans and a dislike for reading anything longer than a friend's most recent blog post. But as in any generation, there are students out there who defy this stereotype. Some even do it proudly. These students can help you get a pulse on what students are really reading. Our club mainly purchases popular books and films for donation to the library, so they let us know when the new book by Zane (a popular romance novelist) is coming out or lobby the group to purchase the hottest anime or graphic novels. Club bibliophiles even promoted the idea of a student book club and managed to get it off the ground. The decision to invite members of the local community, as well as the campus community, was sure to lead to some interesting discussions.

Love of Libraries. Some students just have an interest in libraries. Some club members might have worked as a page in their hometown public library or as an assistant at their school library. If your library uses the Library of Congress call number system, you might find that there is a bit of a learning curve if students are more familiar with Dewey classification, but they'll pick it up quickly enough. Students with an interest in libraries might volunteer their time to shelve books, shelf-read, or do any special projects you might have to offer. If library policy permits, this student might even be able to staff a service point with a little bit of training. You might even find these students are more interested in the task at hand and do a better job than the work-study student you are paying to do the same job. While we admit students like these are rare, they do exist, so stay on the lookout for them.

Student Retention

Involvement on campus is one of the keys to student retention, particularly of first-year students. When students are involved on campus, they develop relationships with faculty, staff and fellow students that improve their experience at the institution. Ideally, students will become involved both socially and intellectually on campus, and will find organizations that match their needs and interests. A library student advisory board can provide a home for students interested in books, reading, intellectual freedom, social awareness and social activity, or just making a difference in their community — with the flexibility to bend in order to meet the particular needs and interests of the membership at any given time.

In *Involvement in Campus Activities and the Retention of First-Year College Students*, Skipper and Argo use research literature to show that a clear connection between student involvement and retention does exist.[28] Furthermore, the essays compiled in the book demonstrate that "a combination of intellectually rich, socially positive, and personally engaging formal and informal campus activities will yield the greatest retention results."[29] While it is unlikely that a single organization will meet all of an individual's social and intellectual needs, a library student advisory board can connect students with common interests and lead to intellectually stimulating discussions during and outside club meetings. The club can also provide members with opportunities to participate in socially positive activities to improve the library, as well as their campus and local community. In addition, club members have the opportunity to form strong bonds with library faculty, staff, and club members in formal club meetings and special events, as well as informal encounters in the library and around campus. Though retaining students for the university is not our primary goal, we do hope the club enriches students' lives.

For a review of the literature on the connection between campus activities and retention, see Skipper and Argo's book.[30] Though it focuses on the first-year student, it often looks at the first-year student in the context of the student body as a whole. Luring new students into the library each year is an issue for most libraries. This makes first-year students a demographic the library needs to attract. New first-year students are a prime segment of the student population from which to recruit new club members. For these reasons, we think anyone interested in developing a library advisory club could benefit from taking a look at this book.

A few chapters that particularly spoke to us and our experience with the club include chapter 2, "Meeting the Changing Needs of Students" and chapter 6, "Developing Curricular and Co-Curricular Leadership Programs." In chapter 2, Schroeder describes his first-year college experience in the early 1960s and uses recent research on college students' academic needs, social patterns, expectations, attitudes and values to illustrate the many ways in which the college experience has changed. While some portray today's students as apathetic and spoiled, research shared in this chapter paints a more optimistic portrait. At the very least, there is a great variety among today's students, and their lives are more complicated than students' lives were nearly half a century ago. The author notes an emerging trend for students — in the light of tighter job markets, the tragedy of September 11 and recognition of the ability to affect change by "thinking globally and acting locally" — to flock to service organizations such as Teach for America and the Peace Corps after college, while student volunteerism tends to drop off somewhat during college.[31] On the lighter side of things, he notes from his own experience, "due to the limited number of personal electrical devices (e.g., radio, clock), two electrical outlets per room were more than adequate" — a terrifying thought for your technophiles![32]

Schroeder argues that to meet students' changing needs and improve the student experience — and thus improve student retention — all student experiences should be tied to education and development. He gives staff working in campus student affairs departments the following advice:

> To become learning-centered, staff in student activities units must shift their current perspectives by (a) viewing themselves as educators; (b) intentionally designing activities and experiences that support and complement the academic mission of their institution; (c) formulating clear and measurable learning outcomes; (d) forging educational partnerships with academic administrators, faculty, and other student affairs educators to promote student learning and success not only *within* their organizational boundaries, but *between* those boundaries and other divisions within the institution.[33]

While we are not staff in the student affairs department and development of such programs is not our primary job, this advice spoke to us because our Library Student Advisory Board is in the beginning stages of accomplishing the exact changes in perspective that were advised by the author. Perhaps this shift in perspective is natural, as the traditional mission of academic libraries is to support the educational mission of the university. The club has been active in building partnerships with faculty to support and organize out-of-class educational activities such as a music festival, dance lessons, and a book discussion group. An area for further development would be to consider discussion of clear and measurable learning outcomes for club activities.

The Library Student Advisory Board

In chapter 6 of the Skipper and Argo book, Dooley and Shellogg discuss student leadership programs. Included are numerous examples of leadership programs and workshops that you may wish to adapt for your own needs. Developing future leaders is part of the mission of many universities, so by encouraging club members to take leadership positions and developing their skills, you are serving the mission of your organization. Club leaders may very well go on to become effective leaders in their professions and their communities. In brief, "encouraging participation and leadership in extracurricular activities helps students feel a part of the institution, develop friendships, and find their place on campus."[34]

The LSAB started as a way to get student input and combat misconceptions with targeted marketing and outreach, but we believe the library and its staff, as well as club members, have benefited in even greater ways. Benefits to the library are described in later chapters, but we do believe that this club meets some of the social and educational needs of the students. Members have the opportunity to work with campus faculty and staff to affect change — integrating them into the campus community. We encourage leadership development and the organization of educational activities of club members' interest. And though we have no concrete data on whether this club has influenced the retention of students at our university, we do believe that together we are taking steps toward making our library more student-centered and integrating students into the campus community.

2

Penn State Schuylkill's Library Student Advisory Board

In this chapter we will share the story of how our club got started, including Marianne's creative recruitment techniques, and demonstrate how the club has proven to be an effective student organization. We will highlight some of the ways the club has benefited the library, the campus community and the local community. Included in this chapter are three essays by past LSAB presidents, Nick Frear, Ashley Fehr, and Loni Picarella. Nick shares his passion for libraries and the Library Student Advisory Board. Ashley briefly provides a student's impression of the academic library, a good reminder that even the smallest academic library is likely to be larger than any school or public library your students have visited in the past. And Loni shares how she has personally benefited from club membership. One of the greatest benefits of club membership for Loni was the friendships created which helped her get through a very difficult time in her life. For all its varied and innovative efforts, the club has duly received recognition in the form of awards and publications. We will conclude by recognizing the students' efforts once again.

How We Started the Library Student Advisory Board

Marianne's Story

After many discussions among the library staff and administration concerning the downward spiral of our library's usage, we decided to try our hand at starting a library-related student club on campus to get some input on why nobody was using this great institution. Once the library decided to try to get a club started, I, Marianne, volunteered to be the club's advisor and started by paying a visit to our student affairs department to get as much information on starting a club as I could. To

21

have a registered club on campus we needed to find eight or more students interested in both joining such a club and petitioning for it to be established. Eight is the magic number at our university — the minimum number of interested students needed to petition for a student club on your campus may be different. Your first step will be to find out the rules and regulations of your governing body regarding the establishment of student clubs. While it would not be necessary to make your library student advisory board a university-sanctioned student club, we have reaped many benefits from going this extra mile. The most significant benefit is funding from the university. There will be more about this later in the chapter.

Your next step will be to find students interested in getting a club started. We expected that it would be a challenge to try to find interested students at the beginning of the school year who would want to take on the responsibility of starting a library club. We also suspected that when students first come to campus at the beginning of a school year the only thing on their minds are their schedules, meeting their roommates, and unpacking — and the general excitement and anxiety surrounding these things. Probably the last thing on their minds is starting a library club. But we wanted to start the club as soon as possible, so over the summer I began by enlisting all of my seventeen-year-old son's high school friends who would be attending the Penn State Schuylkill Campus in the fall. Some of these kids had shared blood, sweat, and tears with my son on the football field for years. Others had spent their weekends at my house playing paintball. When I first started asking them if they would do me a favor and sign up to start a library club, they thought I was joking, and actually laughed at me. And of course I heard the expected, "No, thanks" and "Never! No way!"

Over time, I explained to them how important this was to me and to the library, and begged them to give it a chance. I asked them just to give it a try, just sign their name and come to at least one meeting. I told them that they owed me for all the food I had made them over the years. I had to twist some arms and do a lot of convincing to get them to not only join, but to actually start a library club. Eventually I wore them down. In my case, it helped that they knew I was a good cook. I had cooked for them many times during the paintball and football seasons — and I promised there would be food involved. I explained to them that because the best time for the library club to meet would be at noon, I would provide them with lunch. Knowing how these boys liked to eat, I knew I had won — or they realized how desperate I was.

Though I was just trying to find eight people willing to help get the club started, later we realized I had unintentionally lured in our most evasive patrons. These kids admitted they didn't really like going to the library and usually were thrown out of the libraries in high school for talking or horsing around.

The day of the first meeting was worrisome for me. I paced around the library all morning wondering if these boys would appear. A half hour before the meeting I kept looking out the doors to see if any of them were on their way. I just wasn't sure if they would show up. I was extremely nervous that they would not show and that our idea of a library club would never come to fruition. As promised, there was food — lots of food — prepared by me and other members of the library staff. And when the noon hour finally came I was ecstatic. Not only did they show up, but they arrived on time! They even brought their girlfriends and sisters. We ended up having twelve students attend our first meeting — four more than we needed to get the club started.

We know that such an unlikely, fortunate set of circumstances will not exist for all our readers. But some of you may be in a similar situation, or know someone with a college-age child to help recruit new members. Others may have even greater opportunities to attract a diverse and interested group of students in order to get your club started. The point is, try to look beyond the obvious — solely recruiting the students you regularly see using the library or poaching from your library's work-study student population.

If you don't have a son with a lot of football and paintball buddies to recruit for your club, look to campus students you know in a social context beyond your job — perhaps through a religious or volunteer organization. If you are a regular fan of campus sporting events, try recruiting members of the team or talking about your plan with the coach to see if they have students to recommend. Even if the player is not able to recognize you as a regular enthusiastic team supporter (the home of Penn State football, Beaver Stadium, seats over 107,000 fans), you will have a starting point for your conversation. The same goes for students involved in music, theater, and other artistic pursuits on campus whose events you enjoy attending. When you approach the student, you will not only be able to relate the club to general interests of all students, but the specific interests of that student.

Contact faculty who are library supporters and regularly have their students conduct research at the library to see if they can suggest any students who might be interested in joining your club. In the Internet age, it is entirely possible to have regular and efficient library users who never or rarely step foot in the library or seek assistance from the staff. From these students you might learn what it would take to get them into the library, but you might also learn more about their typical usage of electronic library resources — information that can be difficult to glean accurately from database usage reports.

Try talking with the advisors of other clubs and organizations on campus for suggestions. Or, talk with the staff in your student affairs department. There are always a few students who seem to be involved in everything and might also be interested in getting involved with your club too. These students can give insight into what other groups are doing and have experience with the way other clubs are run, so they can make good officers for your club. These students might also have ideas for fund-raisers and programs based on past experience.

While the above suggestions are hypothetical, not tried and tested methods for recruiting students, we hope they give you some ideas for recruiting an interesting and diverse club membership of your own. We were able to get great ideas and honest feedback from our admittedly most unlikely users — the people we wanted to attract back into the library. We say "back into the library" because though it may have been a long time, you will often find that at one point — maybe when they were very, very young — these kids used to enjoy reading and going to the library with their parents for story time, summer reading programs, or just to borrow books.

Student Reflection on Libraries, the Library Student Advisory Board, and Club Meetings

Nicholas Frear reflects on the important role libraries play in his life and his excitement about being involved with the Penn State Schuylkill Library Student Advisory Board. Nick is currently a sophomore planning to major in meteorology. He became the club president in Spring 2008 after just four short months of membership in the club, but will be leaving Schuylkill after just one semester as president in order to finish his degree program at the University Park campus.

Reflections on Penn State Schuylkill's Library and the Library Student Advisory Board
by Nicholas Frear

I have always considered the library a home away from home. My hometown is a city called Meriden, Connecticut. My grandmother worked at the public library there. When I was little I used to get lost in the book stacks in every part of the library, reading mostly nonfiction books. Meriden was my home for nineteen years, but it's a five-hour drive from Penn State Schuylkill and with no car it's probably no surprise that I hardly go to visit. Now the campus library is my home away from home. The first summer I took classes here you would always find me in the library to escape the heat, boredom, or to write a paper. From the end of my first class of the day till closing time, I was at the library. And I wasn't the only one who considered the library a home. Within no time all the employees and regular patrons like me were part of my Pennsylvania family. It only seemed right that I should apply to work there during the fall. I was always there anyway.

I was already employed at the local CVS drug store and drowning in eighteen college credits, but I still decided to apply to work at the Schuylkill Campus library. I worked as the head cashier at CVS so I had plenty of customer service experience and skills to work at the circulation desk. In fact, it was much easier and enjoyable to help my peers and assist them with their research then to hear the many complaints of CVS customers who never remember their CVS card or coupons.

I guess when I signed up for the library job, I automatically became a member of Mari's Library Student Advisory Board (LSAB). I think it was the home-cooked food served at the meetings that first got me interested in attending. Soon after, I realized how important this board of students was. They were the reason why the whole library seemed like home. The work of the club was something I could really get behind. When the announcement was made that the current president was leaving the campus for bigger and better things, I knew that there would be a need for a new president. I felt that I would make the best candidate for the position. I felt as though I wanted to make the library even more comfortable for everyone. I had many ideas for the library and instead of just suggesting those ideas to the new president, I wanted to be the one to represent LSAB. As soon as I was in place as one of the four candidates I began to brainstorm way of improving this center for leaning. It was a tough campaign to try to influence members that have been there for years that I — a member for only four months — could lead this organization. I have a high GPA. I have two part-time jobs. I was already the secretary of the Gay/Straight Alliance and treasurer of the Nittany Players. Responsibility was nothing new to me.

My perseverance paid off and I was elected president of LSAB! That was like being the head of the household. Out with the old and in with the new. For some reason, even though I hadn't been on this campus for that long, I had some great new ideas for improving the library. In fact, once a week I open my presidential folder I made for LSAB, and behind my copy of the LSAB's constitution I update a list of ideas I would like to share with Mari and the advisory board members. Some include changing the hours for Saturday; instead of opening from 10–3 it should be open from 12–5. I have suggested that the library have an event reminder. I think it would be a great idea to remind students of an event just about to take place by using the library's intercom system. I know I always lose track of time and sometimes I'm just too busy to look up what fun occurrence the campus has to offer today. That's why it is a great idea to have short announcements five minutes before an event starts. I also have some ideas for the library's web page. Some ideas include having a list of newly purchased DVDs available for students. We could also have a top ten movie picks of the week. And one of my favorite suggestions is game night. It was first brought up by one of the members. They suggested an Xbox tournament. I expanded the idea to board games, too. That way more people can be a part of the action. There will be pizza and maybe some prizes — a night of competitive fun!

How the Club Has Been Effective

For what started as a small club at a small university campus, this club has made a significant impact on our library. It has even broadened its horizons to have an impact on our campus, as well as in our local community. Here we will highlight specific ways our advisory board has done that. Former LSAB President Loni Picarella will also share what she views as the personal benefits of club membership.

It's the Thought That Matters

Many of the ways in which the club has made an impact on our library, campus, or community may not seem significant to those with a larger library, an overabundance of discretionary funds, or simply a different student population and campus environment. However, regardless of the overall impact or the actual monetary value of the items donated, the simple acts alone of these students working to improve their library and the library experience for their fellow students are quite significant.

In the five years since its inception, Penn State Schuylkill's Library Student Advisory Board has grown from the nine members who initiated the formation of the club to a cumulative total of 207 members over the club's five years in existence. On average we have thirty to thirty-five members, with about twenty very active in the group. This year, the club's fifth, we have a whopping seventy-one members. Each year we lose fifteen to twenty members at the end of the year due to graduation or transfer to another Penn State campus, and regain about the same number at the beginning of the next year due to recruiting efforts. The club has regular monthly meetings during the fall and spring semesters, typically totaling eight to nine meetings, plus informal meetings of members and participation in special events planned throughout the year.

Finding the Funds

Club members have offered valuable ideas for the library and insight into student life, but have also raised nearly $10,000 to purchase popular books, DVDs, Nintendo Wii and Microsoft Xbox 360 video-game console and games, plus other items to donate to the library. Through a variety of fund-raisers the club has raised nearly $3,600 to purchase materials of student choice for donation to the library. In the early days of the club, fund-raisers considered by members included sales of both candles and makeup, because of members' personal connections to friends and family members selling these items. The club tried the candles, but vetoed the makeup. The candle sales were successful, but candles were later banned from on-campus housing units, which would have stifled future sales. The LSAB then moved on to the sale of long-sleeved T-shirts, scarves, and stadium blankets embroidered with the campus logo. At the time there was a large variety of university paraphernalia available for sale, but nothing bearing the campus name or logo. The club managed to find a niche market, making that fund-raiser such a big success that they decided to do it again the next year. To get some repeat customers and make up for slower sale of the long-sleeved T-shirts and more expensive stadium blankets, the second time members sold scarves and knit caps, both of which were popular fashion accessories at the time.

Less innovative but always popular fund-raisers included candy sales and car washes. All students need to do is carry a box of candy around campus — carrying it with them to class and back home to their dorm or apartment — and the candy practically sells itself. There was always a box in the staff area of the library, and we have to admit we probably bought more than our fair share ourselves. We told the overnight maintenance workers about the candy sale and the box in the library, and most mornings we would find several bars replaced with dollar bills.

Soap, sponges, a couple hours of time, and the willingness to get a little wet are a small investment for a fund-raiser with a large return — a car wash. We were able to use water provided by the campus and a corner of a parking lot, but you might be able to find a local business that will allow you to use their water and parking lot. They may even make a donation to your cause. This provides the business with an opportunity to support the community and they will likely welcome the attention you draw to their business. Our club has been quite successful with simply requesting a donation to the club instead of a set dollar amount for the car wash. And we typically receive larger donations from faculty and staff than students, than one might expect. Another tactic that has helped with our car wash is the valet service for faculty and staff who have class or are unable to get away from their offices during the fund-raiser. On a small campus such as ours, everyone knows each other and most people do not hesitate to hand their car keys over to a colleague — either the club advisor or another library staff member — so their car can be washed and returned to its parking spot. And because it is a small campus, getting someone's keys and moving their car only takes about five minutes. On a large campus with distant parking lots, this service could be time-consuming, but highly valued — one to consider carefully. Finally, a tactic we have seen, but never tried, is to request a donation for a basic car wash and post a set amount for premium services such as tire shine, wax, or carpet vacuum to at least offset the cost of additional supplies. Weather does play a factor in the success of this event; as with any other event being held outside, be prepared with a rain date. We have never had to reschedule, but one year the threat of a rainstorm did slow down traffic at our car wash. Otherwise, the car washes have been so successful that the club quickly decided to make it an annual event.

The club was able to raise a total of nearly $3,600 through these fund-raisers, but over $6,000 of the club's money has come from requests for university funding. Since they form a university-sanctioned student club, the LSAB can apply for monies from the student activities fund generated by the mandatory student activities fee paid by each student, as well as funds from the student government. Requests for funding generated by the student activities fee are reviewed by a committee of faculty, staff, and students. One stipulation is that use of the funds must be for an out-of-class activity open to all students. Also, these funds are not limited to use by university clubs; anyone can make a request to fund an event, spreading the pot a little thinner. In contrast, the student government is allotted a general fund to support club and organization development and it is the members of the student government who vote on these requests for funding. In both cases all requests must be for specific items or events, so it is good for the club generate some ideas at the end of the year about what they would like to request funding for at the beginning of the next. We suspect that many universities will follow a similar structure for the funding of student clubs.

In the five years since its inception, the Library Student Advisory Board has been awarded a total of $6,350 in university funding. While the LSAB has a reputation for responsibly spending funds received, members of the student government are also aware that most funds are used to purchase popular books and DVDs for the benefit of the entire student population. And when members of the LSAB are also members of the student government association they are able to personally persuade fellow student government members of the benefits of approving funds requested by the LSAB. As you can see, the library and the student body has benefited greatly from going the extra mile to make our advisory group a university-sanctioned student club.

Benefit to the Library

With the money received through fund-raisers and university funds the club has not only been able to benefit the library and campus community, but also members of the local community surrounding the campus. As stated above, our interest in a library-related student club was to garner student advice and assistance with getting more students into the library. Due in part to our work with the club, usage of the library is up by as many as 400–500 visits per week in week-by-week comparisons to library usage five years ago. Remember that this is on a campus with just under 1,000 students. The library is still perfecting its relationship with the club, but we have benefited from the advice and library advocacy by club members.

- ADVICE

It is probably no surprise that one of the first recommendations students made was that they would like the library to have a welcoming, comfortable atmosphere. And, of course, the names of a few popular large bookstore chains came up as examples. New furniture wasn't an option at the time, though we hope it will be considered in the future. Things the library administrators were able to do to make the library more appealing to students were to get some soda and snack machines into the library and to diversify leisure–reading magazines by adding subscriptions to a few more men's-interest titles.

When a university libraries task force was seeking input on a new catalog interface, we gave club members a tour of the new features and asked them what they thought. Their responses were then forwarded along with ours back to the task force for consideration. And when we were struggling with finding the best way to inform students about upcoming library events, we polled the club members. In a world where many feel overwhelmed by e-mail, we were afraid that what we viewed as the easiest way to share news of upcoming events would be ignored, deleted, or never seen at all. However, most responded that a general e-mail message at the beginning of the semester, followed by reminders a few days before the event, plus flyers around campus was the best way to get students to attend. Below you will read more about the club's advice to add more color to flyers announcing library workshops in order to make them better able to compete with others on campus bulletin boards. Finally, club members also initiated the establishment of a book club at the library. And people say that kids today don't read.

• ADVOCACY

We did not anticipate that we would benefit from the club through student advocacy for the library, but this is certainly an aspect of our relationship that we would like to develop further. Currently the club members do a great job persuading their friends and classmates to come to the library for the "fun" stuff— the DVDs, books and games they donate to the library. Our challenge is then to take advantage of this opportunity to show students the other things the library has to offer — the educational and intellectually stimulating things.

We have tried to develop students' advocacy for the academic services and collections we provide by informing them of all the things the library has to offer and briefly highlighting features of the print and electronic collections especially relevant to undergraduates. Our challenge with our young group primarily consisting of frosh and sophomores is that many of them haven't had to make use of these things yet themselves. Many don't truly appreciate reference service or massive amounts of information available at their fingertips from anywhere with Internet access because they haven't experienced it yet. Exposing students to research early in their program of study is another challenge altogether.

• EXAMPLES OF LSAB ACTIVITIES BENEFITING THE LIBRARY

Getting Students Into the Library. Among the student body, the most popular contribution by the Library Student Advisory Board to the library are the popular DVDs, bestselling novels, and new Nintendo Wii and Microsoft Xbox 360 game consoles with games for use in the library. In our somewhat rural community the entertainment options are limited, especially for those who have to rely on public transportation. These items provide a temporary diversion when a study break is needed — and they get students into the library. Another simple way the club has helped get more students into the library is by compiling and maintaining a "menu book" of local restaurant menus. Unlike some college towns where you can even order your food online, most of our local restaurants do not have Web sites or include their menus in the local phone book. A simple thing such as this helps establish the library as a source of information relevant to student needs. Once we get students into the library, we have an opportunity to showcase the services and collections we provide. And though it doesn't necessarily help get students into the library, another way the club has enhanced the library's collections is through talented students using their skills to update the campus history archive containing faculty and staff member photographs — something you can read more about in chapter 6.

Another way the Library Student Advisory Board has helped get students to return to the library is by helping with our library open house for new students. Some faculty require attendance at this event as part of their course, so turnout is generally quite good. Over the years the club has helped with nearly every detail of the event, providing a student perspective on theme and content (make it fun, but not childish; make it worth their time, but don't pack in too much), assisting with preparations for the event, and providing a student voice among those of the staff on the day of the open house event. In the past the club has secured funds to purchase supplies and prizes for the open house, as well as popcorn and karaoke CDs (for use with the campus's portable karaoke machine) to help with curbside appeal on the day of the event. We typically get more students than we can manage at one time, so we try to filter them through activities outside the library first so they slowly trickle into the main event. A large crowd outside the building also helps attract others. Library open house participants report that they liked hearing about the library from another student. And since studies show new students often find the academic library intimidating, we hope the involvement of their peers helps reduce any anxiety about the library. For some students the open house is their first time in the library. We believe participation in the events convinces them to return.

Past LSAB President Ashley Fehr's dedication and let's-get-it-done attitude helped the club achieve many things during her tenure. Ashley is an honors student and a 2008 graduate of the Pennsylvania State University with a bachelor's degree in English. Readers will have the opportunity to hear more from Ashley in chapter 9.

Student Reflection on LSAB Members as Library Ambassadors
by Ashley Fehr

In a larger school, the need for such an organization is even more apparent. Starting at a new campus with a gigantic library, even the most avid library fan faces intimidation. While the same Library of Congress organizational system stands, the layout of each place is different. Student ambassadors, like LSAB members, are crucial to provide a student resource. While some students indeed work in the library, their ability to act as tour guides can be limited due to sheer quantities of students and other responsibilities.

In Ciletti, the general collection is kept upstairs while the reference section is downstairs. It was not uncommon for new users to enter the library, skim the reference section looking confused, and start heading for the door. Catching the students before leaving, I would often find that they just wanted to browse the "stacks" and could not find them. Solvable problems like this one are no reason to be losing patrons. Having LSAB members serve as tour guides during open house events to show students the general layout of the building helped to eradicate this problem.

LSAB members forge an important connection between the university life outside of the library and the library itself. Members provide essential communication to a sometimes dauntingly huge body of students that is not always reachable. Flyers, posters, e-mails, and events held outside the physical structure of the library itself are all ways to draw in a crowd.

Finally, club members have promoted a variety of library and club events by preparing and distributing flyers in student housing and around campus. Students recommended that the flyers, typically printed in black on color paper, needed more color to be able to compete with the other posters and flyers on the bulletin boards in order to grab students' attention. To accomplish this, they decided to purchase a color printer with their own funds. Since the library also makes occasional use of the printer, we provide paper and replace the ink cartridges.

Enhancing the Library's Atmosphere. Over the past four years club members have worked to create more than twenty-five READ posters — featuring faculty, staff and students — using one of the CD-ROMs available for purchase from the American Library Association. These posters featuring recognizable faces in the campus community not only serve to promote reading and our library, but helped the club and the library build and strengthen relationships with active members of the faculty, staff, and student body. We were able to have these posters printed on a large printer in the University Libraries' Preservation Department, then mounted to a sturdy backing for quick and easy display changes.

Club members have taken over a library display case across from the library entrance and are committed to monthly, themed book displays corresponding to national holidays, awareness efforts, and campus events. Examples include book displays for National Library Week, Banned Books Week, Constitution Day, Women's History Month, and Black History Month. These book displays are also an opportunity to tie the library into club activities that are not necessarily library-related. We have found that allowing the club's activities to sway with members' interests helps keep involvement in the club high. When club members expressed a desire to sponsor on-campus dances we wondered, what does this have to do with the library? But the club was able to bring the theme of the dance into their book display, integrating the library into the event. Most recently the club sponsored a salsa dance. Not only did they use this theme in their library display, but they also made this an educational opportunity by securing a salsa dance instructor to provide training before the dance.

The club has added a student-centered activity to the library's calendar by starting a book club. The book club was established midway through the spring semester so it was decided members would only read one book before the end of the school year — a trial run to work out the details. Club members worked with library staff to select a few possible titles for their first book, then voted on the selection. The book club meets twice a month and is open to all members of the campus community, as well as the local community. Inviting everyone to participate has lent to a wide diversity of perspectives, making discussions quite interesting. The book club had about six participants at each of the first meetings and it was decided that this was something we should all pursue. The LSAB is in the process of planning a book club schedule for the upcoming year and has selected the final *Harry Potter* book as its first selection. We expect that by choosing a book many students may have read over the summer, when the novel was released, will encourage attendance at the first few meetings of the semester and get students interested in reading the other books selected by the club. We all hope it will be a success and we try to provide as much support as possible. Additionally, the club sponsored and planned another literary event, a poetry slam. This was a first for us and it was amazing to see the talents of our students on display.

Occasionally the club donates other items to the library beyond the popular media items listed elsewhere. After the death of Marianne's mother, a beloved long-time library staff member, the club donated an umbrella stand in her honor. This small item was something Marianne's mother thought the library was in need of for a long time. And while we were celebrating the new library building's tenth anniversary, the club donated one of the stadium blankets they were selling for one of their fund-raisers as the award given to the trivia contest winner. (Answers to the trivia contest questions could be found in the library's county and campus history archives.) In addition, the club donated a tree to be planted on campus to commemorate the anniversary. Moved by this gesture, campus administration also decided to donate two trees.

Benefit to the Campus Community

The books, videos, and games purchased by the club benefit the entire campus community, but we are also proud to have club members representing the library at a variety of campus events each year. Notably, the club was asked by the development office if it would create displays using items from the library's campus history archive to be displayed at a scholarship dinner honoring a retired faculty member. Club members used their artistic skills to create magnificent displays of memorabilia. Dinner attendees enjoyed looking at the displays so much that some stayed late, following the dinner, to take it all in. Others later brought friends into the library to see the displays and stroll down memory lane with former classmates. Perhaps one of these alumni will remember the displays and consider a donation to the library or the club.

Club members have also represented the library by staffing the campus's booth at the local Borough Day event, a day of fun and affordable entertainment for the whole family. Having students, faculty, and staff at the campus booth during the event allows us to place positive representation of the campus into the local community. This also helps establish the club and the library as team players on campus. In addition, students have represented the library and their club by serving as student representatives on Library and Information Systems Committees of the Faculty Senate, providing a student perspective on issues under committee consideration. Finally, club members have helped recruit new students by providing information on student clubs to prospective students and their families during campus open-house events.

Above we mentioned that we have found it is necessary to sway a bit with student interests to keep them involved in the club. Sometimes things the club wants to do are a little difficult to tie to the library. But if nothing else, the club supporting the occasional dance or bus trip helps raise awareness about the club and the library among new and different groups of students. Though local policies prohibited the club from holding a dance as a fund-raiser, the club decided to sponsor a dance anyway. In keeping with the Mardi Gras theme, the club provided beads for the dance and one of the club members volunteered to DJ. This was so successful they decided to do it again. As mentioned earlier, the club also held a salsa-themed dance and integrated the library into it by creating a book display highlighting books on dance and Latin American culture from our collections. A similar tie-in was planned for a bus trip to a local jazz festival.

Benefit to the Local Community

In its third year the club lifted its philanthropic eye to gaze briefly at the world beyond the library. Following the devastation caused on the Gulf Coast by Hurricane Katrina, the club voted to donate $50 to the Red Cross Disaster Relief Fund. The club discussed efforts underway to help rebuild school and public libraries lost in the disaster, but ultimately decided to donate money to be used wherever it was needed most. The group responded again when the family of one of its members was devastated by news of cancer. When the young cousin of a club member — who was more of a brother to her — was diagnosed with a rare form of pediatric cancer, the club responded by sending "get well" wishes and one of the T-shirts they were selling to help boost the boy's spirits. Unfortunately, he was not able to conquer the cancer, but the experience forever linked our student and the club to pediatric cancer causes. Since these events, club members have donated their recipes to a cookbook being sold to raise money for the American Cancer Society, donated in the boy's name. But there was something bigger to come.

While our student and her family were working to fight the cancer, the Library Student Advisory Board just happened to be approached about participating in the Penn State Dance Marathon ("THON") because of the club's reputation for getting things done. You can read more about this in chapter 8 of the book, but the club decided to help raise the funds to sponsor a pair of dancers representing our campus in the 48-hour dance marathon, culminating a year of fund-raising for pediatric cancer. In memory of her cousin who had been lost to the disease, our club member became half of the team of dancers representing our campus at THON. The funds the club contributed were part of the $4.2 million raised by THON that year to provide pediatric cancer care, family support, and research funding.

Though it does not have as wide of an impact as the efforts helping hurricane victims or pediatric cancer families, the LSAB's book club has drawn interest from the community. As mentioned above, the diversity brought to the conversation by the mix of campus faculty, staff, students, and with members of the local community has made for some great conversations. Information about book-club meetings is posted in the local newspaper and we hope this continues to draw interest from the community. Just as we try to make students aware of services and collections our library provides once they are lured into the library by the popular entertainment, we try to be conscious of a making a good impression on the community members visiting the library. For some, it is their first time on our campus.

Student Reflection on Personal Benefits of Club Membership

Past LSAB president and vice president Loni Picarella shares the ways in which she personally benefited from her involvement with the club. Many characterize Loni as a beautiful person, inside and out. While other club leaders' defining characteristic was their enthusiasm, Loni's was heart. Loni put her heart into everything she did and she truly became a loving and caring member of the library family. Loni is a 2007 graduate of the Pennsylvania State University with a bachelor's degree in criminal justice. She currently works at a treatment facility for juvenile offenders.

Lasting Friendships
by Loni Picarella

I have been a member of the LSAB since I was a sophomore in college. The club has given me much throughout my years as a member and officer. I have gained many long-lasting friendships, leadership skills and a solid support system. The LSAB is like a second family to me. I have many positive experiences with the club, but there is one experience in particular that I will never forget.

During my junior year of college I became the vice president of the board. This meant that I would need to be very involved in the club's activities and business. Needless to say, I became very close to the other members and our advisor, Marianne. Something happened that year that would turn my life upside down: my 11-year-old cousin developed cancer. My family was shattered with grief. I took it very hard because Nathan and I were extremely close. I'll always remember getting the horrible phone call because I was at school, in the library, of course. I broke down into a crying mess, my whole body felt numb, and I just did not know what to do or think. Marianne was there at the time and quickly scooped me into her arms and told me it would be okay.

Nathan lost his six-month battle with cancer, but our club never gave up. The LSAB was with him every step of the way. He had cards, T-shirts, stuffed animals and the biggest Penn State fan club ever. My family and I cannot give enough thanks to our club and advisor for all their prayers and thoughtfulness throughout Nathan's illness. From the cards and T-shirts to all the money they raised for Penn State's THON, it is priceless.

To this day the LSAB still supports THON and continues to raise money for children with cancer. Having experienced this myself, I know how much that means to those kids and their families. I could not have gotten through Nathan's death without all of the LSAB's love and support. The club was like a solid rock to lean on when I believed the whole world was crashing down on me. Although our club may not be the biggest one on campus, our hearts are bigger than any numbers on paper. That's the stuff that makes a club amazing; that's the stuff that counts.

Awards

Our Library Student Advisory Board has received some recognition for its innovative efforts. In 2005 the club received a merit award from Pennsylvania Citizens for Better Libraries (PCBL). One of the goals of PCBL is to foster and support local Friends of Libraries groups. Though the LSAB fell outside their definition of a friends group, the PCBL believes the club is building a foundation for lifetime friends volunteerism and was given the award in recognition of their work.

Locally, during the five-year history of the organization, two LSAB presidents have been recipients of the campus Director of Student Affairs Award for Student Organization Improvement. This award recognizes student organizations whose enthusiasm and determination have positively contributed to enhancing the student life and out-of-class experience at the campus.

Spreading the Word

In addition to spreading the news about the club to our local community, we would also like to share what we have learned about working with student advisors with other libraries. Much of what we have learned applies to anyone starting a club on a college campus.

Articles about the club have appeared in the student newspaper, as well as the campus and college library newsletters. Now, the club regularly reports news of events in our campus library newsletter and members often contribute full articles. In addition, the Pennsylvania Citizens for Better Libraries published a photo and reference to the LSAB in their newsletter when the club was honored with their merit award. And an article about the contributions of the club appeared in *College & Research Libraries News*. We have been contacted several times by people who read about the club in one of these publications or found the club's Web site and were interested in learning more. In the following chapters you will read more about what it takes to start a student advisory board at your library and find practical tips based on our experiences.

3

Are You Ready?
Your Job as Advisor

Regardless of why you have become an adviser— be it a role freely chosen or one thrust upon you— an understanding of the challenges and rewards of advising will help you fulfill your responsibilities more effectively.[1]

We are confident you will find that becoming an advisor to any type of club — whether it is a library club, acting club, or a cheerleading club — can be a very rewarding experience. Think of it as a type of adventure, a roller coaster ride, with all its ups and downs, twists and turns. Working with the club we have found that not only have the students grown in their ideas and outlooks, but so have we. Working with the younger generation can be not only a challenge, but also a motivating and uplifting experience. Get to know each of your students as a unique individual, not just as a student. Treat them, their questions, and their ideas with consideration and you will find that your students will return that respect. If you do these things, students will then work hard for the club because they know that you value them as person and consider their thoughts and ideas important to the organization.

Their enthusiasm is contagious and you will often find yourself swept away in the whirlwind created by their vivacity. As the club advisor, Marianne finds herself looking forward to the visits and e-mails that she receives every day, and is reluctant to let them go at the end of the school year. It is likely you will be in touch with your members quite a bit throughout the year, so do try to find the time to stay in touch with your continuing club members over the summer break, too. This will help keep their interest in the club high. As the summer draws to an end and you come closer to the beginning of the new semester, remind your students about the club's first meeting of the new school year. In these e-mail messages, show them your excitement about the upcoming events and let them know of your eagerness to get the new semester started. This way there is a give-and-take of emotion, and your students will come back to campus in the fall excited for another year. Enjoy the experience of being a club advisor.

Since becoming advisor to the library club, my job description has expanded. I,

Marianne Seiler (left), LSAB advisor, with Loni Picarella, 2006–07 LSAB president.

Marianne, now find myself working in a closer relationship with the students than I have in the past, and I am also working directly with other campus departments and clubs. Members drop in unannounced, ask for advice, and hang out at my office. Some of the group's best ideas can come from around my desk when I least expect it.

In this chapter we will discuss the qualities of a good student club leader and developing leadership skills among your student leaders. However, most of this chapter is devoted to the duties of a student club advisor and the importance of having the support of other staff members on campus. Are you ready for the job? As always, we will share ideas that have worked for us. We are confident that if you can commit the time to working with the club, you can do this. See the recommended reading at the end of this chapter for more on advising student clubs.

Are You Ready for a Full-Time Commitment?

To have a successful student club you must be ready to commit your time 24/7 — or at least it feels like that sometimes. A few qualities of a good advisor include being a good listener, allowing and encouraging interruptions during your work day, paying attention to details, being energetic and enthusiastic, having a good rapport with the younger generation, and loving what you do. As one might expect, your job as advisor will be generally to guide the student leaders and help set the course of the club. Duties may include:

- assisting student leaders in understanding and adhering to university policies and procedures
- developing the goals and objectives of the club
- aiding officers with the planning of meetings and functions
- aiding officers with the preparation of funding requests and reports
- coordinating fund-raising efforts
- monitoring club funds with the club treasurer and supervising spending as necessary
- motivating your members
- being available to students to discuss club business or provide a sympathetic ear
- recruiting new club members
- promoting your club and its activities.

An area where students will often need guidance is with understanding and adhering to university policies and procedures pertaining to student clubs. This includes the use of funds allotted by the university and use of university facilities. Though they may not always make sense to your students (and sometimes to you), it is important to ensure that your club is following the policies and procedures established by your university to avoid being penalized for a violation. But, since these policies and procedures have developed over time for the safety of students and to protect the interests of all involved, being familiar with them can also help your club run more smoothly. Keeping up-to-date on policy and procedure changes can be a slippery slope, but this is why having a good relationship with your student affairs department can be extremely helpful. See chapter 5 for more on policies and procedures, and this chapter's "Working with Your Student Affairs Department," page 53, for more on building your relationship with student affairs.

Goals and objectives of your club will be guided by your club's constitution and will generally relate to some aspect of raising awareness about the library, informing the library about student opinion, or raising funds for the purchase of materials of student choice for the library. This gives a lot of room for the club to flex with the interests of its members. One year the focus might be on purchasing gaming equipment, the next it might be creating a book club, or even sponsoring dances with themes highlighted in library displays using your collections. Later, you will even read about the club deciding to give something back for the greater good. See chapter 6 for more about developing and meeting your club's goals and objectives.

The Library Student Advisory Board

Though the direction of the club is not entirely guided by the interests of its members, it is good to find out where members' interests and talents lie. Make a point to discover the talents of your club members. Capitalizing on members' talents makes each one feel they are contributing something valuable to the group. At one of our meetings our campus librarian suggested having the club update our library's archive of faculty and staff accomplishments. While the library had kept up with adding clippings, award programs, and noting significant accomplishments, most photographs hadn't been updated in over ten years and many were missing altogether. We have very talented students who take great pictures and are continually working on this project.

Working one-on-one with your students, you will find out what their passions are, what they want to do with their lives, where they want to go. Building your relationship with your members can improve students' involvement and commitment. We cannot stress enough in this book that you need to know your students, really *know* them. You can't keep them at arm's length — you need to know what is on their minds, how they feel, where their passions lie. As advisor you may find yourself embroiled in your students' lives. This is why it is good for the library to select a "people person" as club advisor. Do not be surprised if you find students often come to you for advice on things other than your library club. Sometimes your students will be missing home, or getting bad test grades, or not getting along with a roommate. When you work with students and take an interest in them, many times they will find you to be a sympathetic ear for their problems. Anyone who has ever worked at a public-service point in a library — reference or circulation — has probably experienced this at some point. In this case you unwittingly develop a relationship with a patron by assisting them and showing them a little kindness. In the case of the club, you might expect that club members will need a sympathetic ear now and then. Remember that you do not need to be a mother, course advisor, and therapist to all these students. Students in need of assistance should be referred to appropriate advising and counseling services on campus. See chapter 6, page 90, below, for more about getting to know your club members and examples of taking advantage of student talents.

Club officers might not realize the importance of having an agenda before going into a meeting. Sometimes students think just having a date and time for the meeting is enough. When you first sit down to discuss and prepare the meeting agenda it might seem like the club doesn't have much to discuss. However, you will often find that the agenda fills out quite quickly with issues to discuss and preparations needing to be made for fund-raisers or other events.

Filling out the same paperwork each year can be a little tedious, but as a constant in the group it is important that you, as advisor, help students anticipate upcoming deadlines for funding requests and regular reports about the club's monthly meetings, events, and activities. In our case funding requests need to be made early in the semester, making it important to discuss plans for the future at the final meetings of the previous semester. One thing I, Marianne, do enjoy is helping students with end-of-year reports highlighting the club's accomplishments. See chapter 5, page 84, "Keeping Good Records," for more on this.

If your club decides to hold fund-raisers, you will need to work with your students to plan and coordinate the fund-raising efforts. We have tried a variety of different fund-raisers. While the potential to easily raise a lot of money — especially in a short amount of time — is a big motivator for the members, the fund-raiser has to be something members are interested in and willing to work to sell. For these reasons, the candy sale was popular and successful, while a suggestion to sell makeup never made it off the ground, and was particularly unpopular with the male members of the club. (Fund-raising will be discussed in more detail in chapter 6.)

As a constant in the group and a responsible adult affiliated with the student organization, it is likely the advisor may play a role in the monitoring of club funds and supervision of spending. These will also likely be duties of the club's treasurer. Together, you will keep track of funds requested, received, and spent, along with the necessary receipts. It may also be necessary to attend occasional budget meetings held by the student affairs department. See "Keeping Good Records" for more.

You need to be able to guide and motivate your members, since many students are only as active as you make them. The key to having a prosperous and thriving club is to keep your students energized and active. Stay in constant communication with your club members through e-mail, phone calls, instant messaging, and stopping to talk when you see them on campus. Be sure to keep updated records of e-mail addresses, home addresses, and phone numbers of your student members so you can keep in contact with them during breaks and summer vacation. When you see club members on campus, go over and talk with them about upcoming meetings, events and activities — or just show your interest in them and ask how their day is going. Taking the time to meet their friends will make a lasting impression and possibly recruit the friends as new members to the club.

As the club advisor, I, Marianne, really have to work to keep the members active. They joke about my overuse of e-mail. I have a tendency to send reminders about upcoming meetings and events numerous times before the actual event; it's almost like a countdown to liftoff. At one meeting I asked for a show of hands of how many members delete my e-mails before reading them. There was much laughter and quite a few hands waving in the air. I now write a reminder in the subject line so even if the student doesn't open my e-mail they know what it is about. For example: "Meeting today at noon!"

Remember to keep your e-mails short and to the point. Students tend to get overwhelmed with e-mail and don't always have (or find) the time to open and read

Library Student Advisory Board members and friends talking about upcoming events.

everything. I make the e-mails colorful and use large print. It is easier on the eyes and fun to read. No matter how many e-mails you send, or how you send them, remember that it works. See chapter 6, page 94, "Motivation," for more on this.

Always make yourself available to your students and continually reinforce the notion that there are no "off the wall" ideas. Make the students feel comfortable by respecting them and their ideas. Treat them as adults and let them know you need them to have a thriving club. Once students get to know you and know that you take them seriously, they will be comfortable sharing ideas and you will find them knocking at your door with ideas, problems and questions, or just to converse. Some of your club's best ideas come from impromptu meetings and brainstorming around your desk, or wherever you happen to run into club members around campus. Keep a pad and pen with you always; you never know when you will be hit with an idea for your club. Ideas can come to you when you're in the least likely spot. After all, fifty years ago who would have thought that there would be coffeehouses with plush chairs, cafés or soda and snack machines, game consoles, and wireless Internet on portable laptops in libraries? See chapter 6, page 107, "Planning for the Future," for more.

Your undergraduates may only be with you a short time, so your membership turnover rate at the end of the year can be surprisingly high and recruiting new students can be somewhat overwhelming. At a small campus such as ours, most students are only here for their first two years of study, and then transfer to another campus to finish their degree. Your club might also experience high turnover due to study

Top: Aleishia King (left), LSAB secretary, and Loni Picarella, LSAB president, standing in front of the LSAB table at the spring 2007 Activities Fair. *Above*: Maureen Ketner signing up students for the Library Club.

LSAB table at fall Activities Fair 2007 (Vince Mitchell, left, senior instructional services specialist and co-advisor for LSAB, with Josh Perreault, vice president of LSAB, 2007).

abroad, scheduling conflicts, or changing interests. Continually recruiting students throughout the year makes it easier to keep up your membership numbers. Having a booth at a campus activity fair is a great way to attract new members. See chapter 7, "Recruit New Members Throughout the Year," for more on this.

Finally, a student club advisor needs to promote the club and its activities. While it is important to promote the club in order to attract new members to the club, is also important to make all students, faculty, and staff aware of what the club is doing. When you have faculty and staff aware of what you are trying to accomplish with your club, you will likely find that they will be supportive and try to work with you. E-mails and phone calls from professors and staff members have already come to us with names of students they felt our club would benefit from having as members. See chapter 7, "Get the Word Out on Campus," for more.

Leadership

The position of club advisor may either be one you take on willingly or a duty you are assigned, but your ability to lead will certainly be tested and expanded during your tenure. As club advisor you will not only be in a leadership position, you will be a model leader developing leadership skills in your members — especially in students voted into leadership positions in the club by their peers. Student leadership skills are expanded when students become interested and involved in campus activities that allow them to reveal their existing talents and skills, while continuing to develop new ones. As Dunkel and Schuh say in their book *Advising Student Groups and Organizations*, "leadership development should not be primarily focused on visible campus student leaders or centered in student government activities; rather, it should be seen as an opportunity to involve many students in activities both on and off campus."[2]

Remind club leaders that they have a responsibility to other club members who look up to them for guidance and direction. Teach your leaders to know members' limitations when it comes to their time and volunteerism, and how to get everyone involved without being forceful. Teach them how to manage people, time, and funds, as well as how to generate good group discussions. Have little workshops for your officers to help build their leadership and communication skills, and also make sure to have students attend any workshops offered by your student government or student affairs department. This helps them come in contact with other student club members and builds their levels of creativity and confidence. Reinforce the idea that your officers need to understand your followers and respectfully listen to each suggestion.

Having observed many leaders over the years and having attended a leadership workshop at some time or another, we have each laid the foundation for the development of our own natural leadership style. Leadership styles range from the leader exerting complete control with little input from subordinates, to delegation of tasks and decisions to trusted members while maintaining the final say in matters and taking responsibility for the outcomes. You will have to choose the leadership style appropriate for your situation based on how much guidance your student leaders need, and possibly how much control library administration and the student affairs department would like you to exert over the club as the group's advisor. You need to strike the right balance of trust and control for your group.

Regardless of your leadership style, we have found the following are some of the essential qualities of a good student club leader:

- having confidence
- being self-motivated
- being able to stimulate conversation within your club
- having decision-making skills (and knowing when to exert them)
- being able to resolve conflicts
- being approachable and taking an interest in all club members' ideas and suggestions

- being a good listener (one of the most important skills of a good leader)
- showing appreciation for members' time and suggestions.

Remember, these qualities not only apply to you as advisor, but the qualities you should look for and develop in your student leaders. There are many ways to help prepare your students for the challenges ahead. Develop students' leadership skills by demonstrating *your* good leadership skills and encouraging them to take advantage of any leadership development opportunities presented to them. It is also good to encourage students to take risks. Even if things don't work out, they can learn from their mistakes. Put students at ease by letting them know that you are there for them whenever they have questions or need a confidence boost. Work together closely in the beginning until they are comfortable with themselves and the duties bestowed on them. See the recommended reading list at the end of this chapter for more information on leadership styles and developing leadership skills.

"A leader's job often includes changing your people's attitudes and behavior," Dale Carnegie wrote. "Praise the slightest improvement and praise every improvement. Be hearty in your approbation and lavish in your praise."[3] We think these words are especially true when working with young people. When you start working with the younger club members, those fresh out of high school, you will notice that many of them are not yet eloquent speakers and few display the confidence to take on the responsibility of a leadership role in the club. You, as advisor, can help them along the way by demonstrating and teaching them the leadership skills they will need to run a successful library student advisory board. However, every so often you have the opportunity to work with students who have the experience and qualities of a leader and are able to step right into a leadership role. Sometimes these students only need a little encouragement from you to get them started.

Creativity Workshop

Our student affairs department regularly hosts workshops for advisors and student leaders. One workshop we found particularly helpful was called "What is Creativity?" At this workshop we learned creative techniques for communicating ideas and helping your club to grow. You could do something similar with your own club. At this workshop we discussed:

- thinking outside the box
- focusing on the positive
- creating a supportive environment
- having fun

A beautiful day on the mall walk for the fall 2007 Activities Fair at Penn State Schuylkill.

- sharing a "victory log"
- delegating work to help your club grow.

In an article in *CanadaOne* magazine, Ed Bernacki writes, "Out-of-the box thinkers know that new ideas need nurturing and support. They also know that having an idea is good but acting on it is more important. Results are what count."[4] Thinking outside the box is one of our favorite concepts. You can just let your imagination run wild and the possibilities are limitless. At the beginning of the year, try to have a brainstorming session with your members. The students really get into this exercise. Ask your club members to take a piece of paper or use a flip-chart, blackboard, or whatever you have handy, and have your students write down any off the wall, never-before-done, creative ideas. Have them use bright colors. Explain to everyone that this exercise is not a time to be negative or critical. Have them listen to each other's ideas and be supportive. Have fun with this exercise and you will be astonished that a single word, phrase, picture, or idea can actually turn into something big.

A practical tip we picked up at the workshop was the idea of a "victory log." At several points throughout the year, have club members discuss the group's accomplishments during that year. This reminds members that they are making a difference and encourages them to continue their efforts. Ask club members to create a

Ashley Fehr (left), past president of the LSAB, and Susan Martin, library staff assistant, working on the LSAB's Victory Log.

colorful scrapbook, or victory log, including pictures of members at meetings, special events, and so on. Include the flyers club members made and any programs they might have done. You don't necessarily need a fancy scrapbook; a three-ring binder works just as well. Have your students date the entries and when the binder is filled simply start a new one. What a legacy to look back on years down the road. New members will also enjoy looking over the victory logs of past years and may even start to think of ways to outdo the efforts of members in previous years.

A final tip from the workshop that we really took to heart was a reminder about the importance of delegating work to help make your club grow. As advisor, you play a role in ensuring that work is evenly distributed among the members as much as possible—and also that you don't end up doing all the work. There will be times when you won't get any volunteers, so it will be up to you to decide who you think would be good for the job. Often times there are students who would like to help but are too timid to volunteer. As you get to know your students a little better, you will come to know what their likes and dislikes are. If the task might be too large for one individual, delegate the job to a group of students and put one of the club members in charge. You will find that students will accept the responsibility given to them,

PENNSTATE Capital College

Libraries News

PENN STATE HARRISBURG
PENN STATE SCHUYLKILL

Volume 13, Issue 3, Fall 2004 • Published for Capital College Libraries Users

Timeline

1987-88. Fund-raising throughout Schuylkill County results in donations of $1.1 million from private businesses and county residents for construction of the new building. Gov. Robert P. Casey allots $1.6 million in state funds.

July 11, 1991. Dedication of the future site of the Ciletti Memorial Library. Pennsylvania National Bank (now M&T Bank) donates the painting, *Nesho Allen Discovering Coal*, by George Luks, to the new library.

July 15, 1993. Groundbreaking ceremony for new building.

Dec. 16, 1994. Occupation of the completed Ciletti Memorial Library begins. Volunteers move 31,000 books in under seven hours.

March 3, 1995. Following restoration and reframing, Luks's painting is installed.

April 13, 1995. Dedication of the Ciletti Memorial Library.

Ciletti Library 10th Anniversary Planning Underway

by Amy L. Deuink

Planning for the 10th anniversary of the Ciletti Memorial Library – Schuylkill County's leading academic library – is now underway. Director of Capital College Libraries Harold Shill, Campus Librarian Wes Loder, and Ciletti Library staff have been meeting with Campus Executive Officer Sylvester Kohut, Jr., Assistant Dean for Academic Affairs Patti Mills, Director of Development Jane Zintak, Manager of Public Information and Publications Steve Hevner, and Assistant Director of Alumni Relations Laurie Dobrosky to plan the anniversary event, which coincides with an effort to raise monies to expand the library's book collections and improve availability of new technologies. A representative of the campus Library Student Advisory Board will contribute a student's perspective to the planning.

The event is tentatively scheduled for April 21, 2005, the 10th anniversary of the original dedication of the building. The celebration will begin early in the afternoon, following the Schuylkill Campus Advisory Board meeting, which will permit Penn State Schuylkill's most supportive

Continued on page 2

Ciletti Library 10th Anniversary Planning Underway

Continued from page 1

community advocates to attend. The possibility of holding smaller events throughout the semester to lead up to the celebration day is also being discussed. The library's decennial year coincides with the 70th anniversary of the Penn State Schuylkill campus, the 100th birthday of Schuylkill County's most famous author, John O'Hara, and the 150th anniversary of The Pennsylvania State University.

Photo by Wes Loder

Scrapbook page created by Susan Martin and Ashley Fehr.

The Library Student Advisory Board

Spotlight on Student Workers...   Ashley Fehr

Ashley is a junior English major from the Pine Grove area. This is her first year working in the library, although she has been a dedicated library user throughout her years at Penn State Schuylkill.

Ashley's many activities keep her always on the go. On campus, she is the president of the Library Student Advisory Board (LSAB), a member of the THON committee and Commuter Council, and a former SGA senator. She also is employed at the Red Lion Café.

Ashley says she enjoys studying in the Ciletti Library because of its intimate, friendly atmosphere, and she contributes greatly to that atmosphere when's she's behind the desk. Thanks, Ashley, for your enthusiasm and willingness to go the extra mile!

We'll miss Ashley as she leaves for University Park in the fall to complete her degree and pursue her dream of becoming an English professor and/or a famous novelist. Who knows, someday we may have her books on our shelves!

Scrapbook page created by Susan Martin and Ashley Fehr.

but remember to be supportive and offer help when needed to encourage the group to get the job done.

> *The difference between "involvement" and "commitment"*
> *is like an eggs-and-ham breakfast: the chicken was "involved"—*
> *the pig was "committed."— Unknown*

Get Help from Other Staff Members

As your club grows, so do the work and responsibilities. It helps to have others lending a helping hand when needed. To avoid burning yourself out, especially while your club is getting started, enlist your fellow workers for any kind of help they can offer — whether it is with paperwork, discussing ideas and suggestions, recruiting new members, or making food for the meetings (see chapter 4, "What Shall I Serve?"). We hope that you will find that your library's staff members will become as excited about the club as you and your club members. We have found that other staff members at our library also look forward to the club meetings and have come to enjoy the friendship of the students as much as we have. Having other staff members with an interest in the club can be invaluable to you in times of need.

To have a successful club the students must sense unity within your library so that if the club advisor is not available your students will not hesitate to go to another staff member with a problem, question, or idea. Remember to always thank your fellow workers and let them know how much their contributions help to make the club a success. And while we are talking about appreciation, when one of our staff members purchased additional DVDs to add to the library's collection, we sent out an e-mail letting the club members know that she had been inspired by the club's activities and suggested that they thank her for her contributions. We send out thank-you cards to everyone for their donations to the library. Finally, each donation receives a bookplate to let patrons know that this particular item was purchased by or in honor of someone. Many of you probably already do this to let people know how much the library appreciates their donations and support.

Reaping the Benefits of the Seeds You Sow

The time and effort you and other library staff members put into improving students' experience with the library will be returned. All students need to see friendly and welcoming faces in the library or they may be turned off by their experience and hesitate to return. When students see the library as a comfortable and relaxed environment and feel it is a student space, they will continue to return. And not just for studying, meeting with classmates and friends, or for relaxing, but for much-needed research help. Many students feel intimidated by libraries and are afraid to ask library staff for help, but when they see the relaxed atmosphere and friendly faces they are often more comfortable and apt to approach the staff for help.

Our club members are often in the library just hanging out or studying, and if they see a student who looks like they are in need of assistance, they don't hesitate to ask if they need help. As trained library advocates, sometimes they are able to help the student themselves, other times they seek out a staff member for assistance. It is great to have dedicated club members who can take a little bit of the burden off library workers and lend a hand at times when there may be a line of students waiting to ask for help. You might even find your club members will volunteer in the everyday workings of the library.

On other occasions we have asked the club members to give tours of the library to potential or incoming first-year students. It may have happened due to the fact that the staff was stretched a little thin that particular day, but we find the students on the tour often seem to be more interested in what a peer has to say. We coach the tour guides on what information we would like them to share on the tour, but they always put their own spin on it and throw in little bits of information that offer insight only another student would have. If you would like to expand on this club

Tiffany Cresswell-Yeager, assistant director of student affairs.

activity, see if your college or university has a "student ambassadors" group that gives tours of the campus and use them as a guide in developing your own program.

Working with Your Student Affairs Department

If you want your club to be successful we feel that you *must* have an excellent relationship with the staff in your campus' student affairs department. We believe our club would not have been such a success without this relationship.

Our assistant director of student affairs, Tiffany Cresswell-Yeager, has been a tremendous help and friend to our Library Student Advisory Board since the beginning. In a discussion with Tiffany about keeping club members active and the group successful, a few of the words that really struck us were: passion, commitment, communication, energy, student values, proper training, motivation, and strong advisor. Tiffany commented, "I tell the students we don't want 'Secret Agents.'" Communicate to your students that one of club's goals is to spread the word about the club and what the club does. If your club is a secret you won't be able to recruit new members because no one will know about you and what you do. Pamphlets, flyers, word of mouth, members getting their friends involved, posters, displays, and e-mails will all help you recruit new members.

Attend Student Affairs' Meetings for Student Clubs

All campus clubs share the common goal of enriching the student experience. It is well known that students learn more when they are involved in a variety of activities both inside and outside of class.

In order to keep all club advisors and student leaders on track, your institution's student affairs department will likely hold occasional meetings and training sessions for you. An example of a creativity workshop we found particularly helpful was mentioned above. These workshops will give you a chance to meet and network with other club advisors and student officers when attending student affairs budget, financial planning and policy meetings. Don't be afraid to ask questions and make sure to share your ideas, goals, and achievements.

In our case, these meetings usually start with an introduction of all members and a description of one project they would like to accomplish for the semester. Students talked about raising money for bus trips to special events and museums, holding a concert featuring student musicians, and raising funds to produce a play. This gives us advance knowledge of upcoming events and gives us insight into clubs we might collaborate with to raise student awareness about the library. You will be astounded by how many new ideas you will get for your own club.

When we attend these meetings we like to invite the officers and advisors from other clubs to visit and sit in on the LSAB's monthly meetings. This will give the other organizations the opportunity to tell your club members about their organization and provides an opportunity for clubs to exchange ideas. Ideally, opportunities for collaboration will develop, providing ways to help each other to grow. See chapter 5 for more on student club-related policies and procedures.

Recommended Reading

Cress, Christine M., Helen S. Astin, Kathleen Zimmerman-Oster, and John C. Burkhardt. "Developmental Outcomes of College Students' Involvement in Leadership Activities." *Journal of College Student Development* 42, no. 1 (January/February 2001): 15–27.

Longitudinal data from 875 students at ten institutions were analyzed for the impact of student participation in leadership education and training programs on their overall educational and personal development. Results showed that students did experience growth in their leadership skills, as well as civic responsibility, multicultural awareness, understanding of leadership theories and personal and societal values. This article could be used to build a case for the necessity of providing leadership training and leadership opportunities for students.

Dunkel, Norbert W., and John H. Schuh. *Advising Student Groups & Organizations.* San Francisco, CA: Jossey-Bass, 1998.

This book is an excellent reference for all clubs. It covers financial management, dealing with conflict, and roles and functions of advisors.

Komives, Susan R., Julie E. Owen, Susan D. Longerbeam, Felicia C. Mainella, and Laura Osteen. "Developing a Leadership Identity: A Grounded Theory." *Journal of College Student Development* 46, no. 6 (November/December 2005): 593–611.

This research article explores students' development of their leadership identity. It is an interesting read for new advisors or advisors in a new leadership position in the process of developing their own leadership identity.

Morrison, James L., Jo Rha, and Audrey Helfman. "Learning Awareness, Student Engagement, and Change: A Transformation in Leadership Development." *Journal of Education for Business* 79, no. 1 (September/October 2003): 11–17.

The authors conclude that real-life leadership scenarios are an effective means of leadership development and that students recognize the educational value. This is an interesting article for new advisors.

Yukl, Gary A. *Leadership in Organizations.* **Upper Saddle River, NJ: Pearson/ Prentice Hall, 2006.**

Although this book leans toward leadership in a managerial sense, it gives wonderful insight into how you personally can improve your skills as a leader in any undertaking that you pursue.

4

Starting Your Own Library Student Advisory Board

Once you decide you want to start a library student advisory board, you need to start asking some questions about what it takes to get a club started. You should recruit a few willing students to help you with this — since the organization will be a student club. If you're not ready for a formal, university-sanctioned student organization, getting an informal advisory group established will be easier. However, it may be more difficult to recruit new members for the club when you are not involved with student-club-related activities organized by your student affairs department. Also, it may be less likely that you will qualify for university funding. Additional benefits we have reaped from having a university-sanctioned student organization are described in chapter 2.

In this chapter we will discuss some common requirements for establishing a new student club on campus and reiterate the importance of establishing a good working relationship with the staff in your student affairs department to achieve your club's goals. We will discuss recruiting the first students needed to establish your club's core membership and share a student's perspective on the library to help convey to students the reasons why they might want to get involved with a library advisory club. In this section, former Library Student Advisory Board President Patrick J. Troutman shares his initial impression of our library, why he wanted to get involved with the LSAB, and what he gained from his experience with the club. We will conclude with a discussion of how to run those first few meetings in a way that attracts new students, helps them become comfortable working with each other, and makes at least a few of them desire to become leaders in the group. Here you will have the opportunity to read a reflection by past LSAB president Hannah Tracy, on her excitement upon finding a library club on campus and her involvement with the club. See the recommended reading list at the end of this chapter for further information on traditional academic library friends groups.

Anyone thinking of starting a club needs to ask themselves a few serious questions:

- Why do you want to start a library club?

- What do you want your club to accomplish?
- How much work can you put into a club?
- Who would do the best job as advisor for your club?
- Will you be able to get students interested?

Once you and your library have made the commitment, you will also need to consider ideas for naming the club and how frequently the group will meet, among other details. Again, if possible, try to get the input and assistance of a few students interested in getting such a club started.

We wanted to get students back into our library and thought an active group of student advisors could help. We hoped students could provide us with input on exactly why it was that few students were using our library — and ideas on how to change that fact. What were their impressions? Considering we live in a society where "Google" is a verb, did they consider the library at all when given a research assignment? Did they think of us when looking for a place to study or meet with a group? Did they realize that our computers and wireless Internet access gave them an alternative to computer labs or a noisy dorm room? Did they realize that we were there to help them succeed? We wanted and needed student input to see what it would take to get them back into the library. We needed a library student advisory board.

We decided to get a club started, but no one realized at the time just how much work the club would be. However, Marianne (our club's advisor) is very passionate about the club and encourages — maybe even pushes — club members to follow through on their ideas. Maybe she does a little bit more work than your average student club advisor, but she certainly doesn't let members slack. The library has a vested interest in seeing this club succeed, making Marianne more than an advisor. She is a liaison and a leader. Her passion for the club and sharing the wealth contained within a library is contagious. I, Amy, believe it is what has made our club so successful. It wouldn't be the same without a leader in the library who cared so much for the club and the students involved. That said, we recommend that you decide up front how much time your advisor will have to commit to the club and if the goals you hope your club will accomplish can be achieved in that period of time. We encourage the advisor to seek help from other library staff members when needed — in a small library such as ours we are always lending each other a hand. Make sure the person selected as advisor has approval from supervisors to regularly devote a portion of the workweek to club activities.

After a few meetings with library faculty and staff we decided to create a library club and appoint Marianne as the club's advisor. In our case, she was the natural choice because she was already so enthusiastic about our library and sharing it with students. We find that qualities of a good club advisor include:

- Being a "people" person
- Being enthusiastic and energetic
- Being a good listener; permitting and encouraging interruptions during your work day
- Having a good rapport with younger generations, or getting along well with students
- Having an open mind
- Having an attention for detail.

Be sure to select someone who will enjoy the work necessary to get the club off the ground and lead it to success. For more about an advisor's duties, see chapter 3.

Once you decide to start your club, you need to select a name. We decided to give our club a distinguished-sounding name because these students will be working with faculty and staff to strengthen the library. Our library staff went over many possibilities and decided on *Library Student Advisory Board*, or, as we fondly call it, LSAB. Some clubs on campus have fund-raisers to go on trips and to make money for fun activities, but our library club advises the leaders of a historic institution on ways to further improve and raises money for the library and the campus community. On our campus, our club is the only one that benefits the entire campus community, not just the members involved.

Get the Facts

After you decide to take on a library club, meet with someone from your student affairs or student activities department on campus and explain to them just what it is you want to do. Be sure your student leaders are also in attendance. The student affairs department should have all the information you need to get your club recognized by your university. Requirements will vary by university, so rather than simply report the steps we had to take, we investigated the requirements for starting a student club at ten universities. A sample of those requirements follows.

- The minimum number of members required to establish a new and unique student club ranges from four to ten.
- At one university a club advisor is optional and at another it is permissible for a graduate student to advise an undergraduate club. Typically, either a university faculty or staff member may be a club advisor. In some cases an advisor must be a faculty member. At least one university requires the advisor to sign an agreement regarding their participation in the club. Another requires advisors to attending training every three years.

- Most universities require each club to have a constitution and/or mission statement.

- Most require accurate contact information be kept on file with the student affairs department and/or the student government.

- Some were not clear about the approval process in their external documentation, but on the university Web sites on which we could find this information it was common for clubs to simply register with student affairs and/or the student government to become recognized as a student club. Some also required a formal petition and review process in the student government. This is true in our case.

- At some universities you may need to register each year to remain an active club.

- Some universities automatically give clubs "seed money," once officially recognized, to help get the club started.

- One university required a petition signed by at least sixty students showing student support for the club; petitioners did not necessarily need to join the club.

- One university required that no more than one-third of the active members be unaffiliated with the university (neither faculty, staff, student, nor alumnus) and it strongly encouraged that the club be student-run.

Constitution

As shown above, it is likely that your club will have to develop a constitution to be approved as an organized student club. If your club needs to establish a constitution, the staff in the student affairs department should have a sample of a basic template to follow and adapt for your organization. Included here is a sample constitution from our club. As you can see, this process will probably be quite simple.

Constitution

Name: Library Student Advisory Board (LSAB)

Purpose: The purpose of this organization is to promote student input and involvement in library services and programming.

Officers: President shall be responsible for delegating authority and representing the organization at student government meetings. Also, the president will preside at all meeting and events.

Vice President shall be responsible for coordinating programs and to oversee organizational activities in the absence of the President.

Secretary will record minutes at all organization meetings and will be responsible for maintaining accurate record of all organization business.

Treasurer will be responsible for all financial recording and balancing the account through student activities. The treasurer will be responsible for all financial concerns in the organization.

Membership: Membership in this organization is open to any student of the Penn State Schuylkill Campus.

Advisor: The advisor will provide guidance and consultation for organization's events, programs, and activities to determine that organizational activities are within the policy of the university.

Elections: Officers will be elected the first week of April.

Voting: All active members will have voting rights, except for organization president and advisor. An active member is one who has attended a majority of events and meetings. Amendments will be passed by a ⅔ majority vote.

Establish a Good Relationship with the Student Affairs Department

Create a firm foundation for your new club by working closely with your student affairs department, particularly with anyone with responsibility for student clubs. As described in chapter 3, a good working relationship with these individuals can be very beneficial to your club and its advisor. Once your club is established, build a good relationship by inviting student affairs staff members you frequently work with to one of your meetings. As an advisory group, your club might be quite different from others on campus. Show them what your club is about and demonstrate what you want to accomplish for your library and campus community. With their insider knowledge, they may be able to help match your club to funding or collaboration opportunities.

Time to Twist Arms — Recruiting New Members

I, Marianne, was really nervous before our very first meeting of the LSAB. Was I well enough prepared? Would the kids take me seriously? Would this club work? Would we be able to get more students, staff, and faculty to use the library? My mind went round and round and I couldn't sleep the night before. I knew what kind of club we wanted for our library and I had an outline of what I wanted to discuss, but I was unsure how it would go. Many students stay away from the library unless they absolutely have to be in one. Have a plan of action and specific goals that you would like to discuss at your first meeting. Being well prepared for that first meeting will help you stay calm and cool.

Our first club members were not exactly what you would call typical library users.

We needed to have eight members to establish a student club. I was very excited and wanted to start the club as soon as possible, so I enlisted (or coerced) my son's friends planning to come to Penn State Schuylkill in the fall. I had known these boys from my son's football team for a few years and many of them had spent summers and weekends swimming and playing paintball at my house. Believe me, I had to twist arms. I had to beg them many times and bribe them with food, but finally they agreed. Libraries definitely were not on their agendas and I wasn't even sure if I could get them to show up. The big day came and I was pleasantly surprised — no, shocked — that they came and even arrived on time. A few even brought their girl-friends, and one member brought his sister.

We started our meeting with our typical joking and teasing, but quickly moved on to brainstorming. I wanted to know what they wanted in their library and what would get them into the library. I was totally amazed by the answers and the great suggestions that they had. The guys wanted to read men's magazines and sports magazines. They said they like to eat and drink when they study and you can't do that in a library. One of the guys said, "I get yelled at the high school library when I talk with my friends." It took some coaxing to get the girls to open up. They didn't say much during that first meeting, but they also didn't know me like the boys did. This first cohort of club members worked extremely well together because most had grown up together in a small town and played football as a group all through school. What we had to do now was get new members involved with this close-knit group.

Accomplishing this wasn't as hard as expected and it didn't take long until other students wondered about the club and what we did. The boys were friendly, loud, and sociable, drawing attention to themselves and the group. And I was aggressive about recruiting, taking any chance I got to tell new students about the club and asking them to join. Every time a student asked about the club I signed them up. When a student came up to the circulation desk I asked them if they heard about the club and were they interested in joining. When we had library open houses, I talked to potential members about the club and had sign-up sheets ready. I gave out colorful handouts and my business card to anyone who would take them. When the parents came with their sons and daughters, remarking on how beautiful our library was, I didn't hesitate to talk about the club and how our members helped in making our library great. I also signed up our library student workers who showed an interest in the club. No matter where I was on campus, if I saw a student, I would try to sign them up.

Once these students understood we wanted them here and we were really serious about understanding what they wanted in a library, they opened up and worked extremely well with us. When the club started to have an effect on the library, our usage started growing, and so did membership in our club. I recruited students any time I had the chance, mainly through encounters with students in the library and around campus. By the end of the first year we had nineteen students involved.

Since that tenuous first semester we have started to participate in the campus activity fair, essentially a market for student clubs. Once each semester students have the opportunity to "shop" for clubs that match their interests and that they might be interested in joining. You can read more about our recruitment efforts in chapter 7.

Hip to Be Square — A Library for Everyone

A library that has a student advisory board is a library that is thinking of its future. Our libraries should be filled with dichotomies; for example, traditional reading rooms with wireless Internet access and plenty of outlets. Rather than just change, we should keep old traditions while developing new. We need to embrace both our traditional stereotype (think Librarian Action Figure, with "Amazing Shushing Action"[1]) and that of the new-age hipster librarian.[2] We need to have the traditional quiet places to study and places where students can talk and play games without disturbing others. We need to maintain structure and order, while having the capacity to be flexible. Updating images are a common marketing strategy. Long-time users recognize small changes and new users are attracted to the modern image. What students seem to want is a library for everyone.

Our library club is a mixture of all types of students. We have traditional college-age students and adult students. We have students from all races and from different walks of life. We now have hometown students and students from Africa. We have the overachievers; athletes; quiet, studious types; and the students still trying to figure out just who they are. All of these personalities are what make for fabulous club. What a good club needs are new and innovative ideas to make the library a place to suit every personality.

Different students are interested in different things. Some of our club members' suggestions are for more men's and women's magazines — non-academic, please! DVDs that they can check out for free, best-selling books like suspense stories and murder mysteries that take minds off everyday studies. "Could we please drink a soda or coffee when we study, or eat a pack of crackers?" "I would like a poetry reading to show off my writing." "To make some money for the club, let's have a softball game, faculty and staff against the students." "We need a new printer, the printer we have is always broken down and in need of repair." These are only a few of the ideas and suggestions we have had during our meetings.

It had been difficult for the library to justify purchase of entertainment media for students by sacrificing academic titles. This very first meeting was the origin of the club's decision to raise money in order to purchase entertainment materials for donation to the library. Once we get students attracted to these items into the library, the burden is on the library to market our academic collections and services.

Once your students have their first meeting they will be eager to come back for the next one. You will find that they won't even wait until the next get-together before they are knocking at your door to tell you about a new idea or something they couldn't wait until that next gathering to tell you. We find that when you have a diverse group of students with different interests, you get so much more out of your meetings than if everyone is of the same opinion. Discussion and disagreements and different points of view — these are what keep your club well-rounded and interesting.

Libraries need to both embrace their stereotype, to keep traditional users, and break away from it, to attract new. You don't have to be a certain type of person to use the library. Libraries are not just for the creaky, dusty old librarian who smells of mothballs and quiet, mousy students. Libraries of the twenty-first century should appeal to everyone. Internet, gigabytes, USB, LCD, wireless, laptops, wikis, blogs, social networking, social bookmarking, DVDs, DVRs, Xbox 360, Playstation 2, Wii, espresso, cappuccino, latte, chai, biscotti: does this sound like Melvil Dewey's library? If you don't keep up you will fall behind; this is so true of libraries of today. Times are changing and libraries have to adapt along with the rest of the world or they will be left behind. You need to meet students' expectations for a traditional library in a way that works with their twenty-first-century lifestyles. Today you need more than books to keep your students and patrons happy. Most of us are trying to do this, but seeing our efforts through the eyes of a student can be enlightening.

Student Reflection on Making the Library a Welcome Place for Everyone

Patrick J. Troutman reflects on his initial impression of the library and experience with the Library Student Advisory Board. Patrick was an early and enthusiastic member of the club and eventually was elected president. His charm and his enthusiasm for the club and library attracted many students to the group. He is a December 2007 graduate of Pennsylvania State University with a bachelor's degree in English.

A Library for Everyone
by Patrick J. Troutman

When I first came to Penn State — Schuylkill as a bright-eyed, eager freshman I was not just looking for an education; I was looking for a job. Sparked by my love of literature, my first and only choice was a job at the campus's Ciletti Memorial Library.

My first experience at the Ciletti was early in the semester when I approached the main circulation desk in search of an application. There, I met the library's receptionist, Ann Snyder. Ann seemed to be the sweetest, kindest woman imaginable and it was then that I knew I needed to work there. I felt immediately at home when Ann smiled and gave me an application.

A week later, I was hired as a library aide in charge of shelf maintenance and clerical duties. I found the library to be a rather friendly and easy-going place. The staff was instantly eager to welcome me. One problem that I did notice, however, was the lack of students using the library for leisure, or merely to pass the time. For the most part, students would use the library solely for research purposes and last-minute studying, which is great, but I'd sort of hoped that there'd be a bit more social activity going on. Despite the friendly staff, the library just seemed to be a business-as-usual environment.

And then I met Marianne Seiler.

One day I asked Marianne—or Mari, as she is called—about her newly formed Library Student Advisory Board (LSAB). She instantly signed me up, saying that the club needed as many bright-eyed students as possible. The club's concept intrigued me. Mari had an idea that would help to change the library's image and make it a more welcoming and accommodating site on campus for all students.

The first LSAB meeting that I attended involved a brainstorming of ideas on how to get more students active, not only in library use, but in the club itself. The club's membership at the time consisted mainly of students who lived in the area and commuted daily. A small number of students who lived in the on-campus housing were also involved, mainly because they also held work-study positions in the library. I was a commuter, as well as one of three library employees involved in the club. This mix of students was a major factor in gaining club members and spreading the word around campus about what the club was doing.

The club realized that one way to spread interest was to get the students involved in what the library was doing. An expansion of the library's movie collection was needed, in order to stay up to date with the ever-growing popularity of DVDs. The LSAB created an on-campus movie poll to let students vote for the movies they wanted available in the library. The interest that students showed with this poll gave the LSAB confidence that student involvement could be easily achieved. All we needed to do was make the students realize that their input was appreciated and implemented.

The movie poll was my first big project with the LSAB. I realized that projects like these had not been done before on this campus. The idea that we were breaking new ground made me really excited to do more with the club. When friends of mine, who were not associated with the club, started asking me about it, I was more than willing to give them information about how they could get involved.

Students began to actively make suggestions for ways to make the library more welcoming. I was really pleased to see soda machines installed in the library's café where coffee had previously been the only refreshment. The library's decision to lift the rule prohibiting food and drinks gave the students fewer restrictions and a more relaxed atmosphere to do their work. In no time at all, students began to use the library as an escape from the noisy campus cafeteria. I was proud to see that the library's atmosphere was already beginning to change for the better. Allowing students to eat their lunch *and* do their work proved to be a huge draw in increasing library use.

As the year went on, more and more students became aware of the LSAB and what we were doing. My fellow student workers, as well as the library's faculty and staff, began to grow more involved in the club's activities. This added support was incredibly helpful in broadening the club's reach. The student workers became more knowledgeable of what the club was doing. This allowed them to spread the word to library patrons, which included students, as well as campus faculty. The library's faculty and staff, including Amy Deuink, the reference librarian, did similar work by spreading the word to other Penn State campuses.

The word of mouth that was spreading throughout the campus and university was a highly effective way to let the Penn State campuses know what we were doing. Penn State–Harrisburg[3] became a prominent benefactor in helping the LSAB achieve its goals. All of this support allowed our club to gain a positive reputation and a greater platform to appeal to all types of patrons.

As the school year drew to a close, I was elected president of the club. I was thrilled and so, so proud. Mari and I became close friends through many brainstorming sessions throughout the summer, during which I remained a student worker. I needed to keep myself closely involved in the decisions and ideas that formulated. Working with the club became a great passion of mine and I was determined to make even more positive changes. I knew that bringing more people into the library was only half the battle. The library needed to offer more incentives than refreshments and snacks.

It became clear that Penn State was taking our club seriously when Mari got a call from our assistant director of student affairs. I was invited to join other student organizations at the Penn State Leadership Conference, in Seven Springs, Pennsylvania, as a representative of the Library Student Advisory Board. The conference was something that I was honestly apprehensive about. I was going to be going joining the other students from Schuylkill as well as meeting hundreds of others from all of the other Penn State campuses. This was rather intimidating to me.

At the conference, I met with a lot of PSU students from all over the state and informed them about the LSAB and our goals. I was not surprised to find that the majority of the students had no idea that the libraries were such a progressive institution. I was an ambassador to the world of Penn State, sent to spread the news of the club's great ideas and innovations. By the end of the conference, all intimidation was a memory. Everyone from Penn State was so friendly and so willing to be themselves and share their ideas. On my way home, the first person I called was not my mom or my dad, but Mari, to let her know how amazing our club was going to become.

At the start of my sophomore year, the club celebrated its first full year of existence. Working with other organizations at the leadership conference made me realize what further steps we needed to take. I became a member of the Student Government Association, or SGA, in order to oversee all of the decision-making that went on at Penn State — Schuylkill. I was able to apply the SGA's strategies, as well as the problem-solving tactics learned at the conference, to my own work as president.

My main goal as the club's president was to continue to make the library a more accessible place for the campus and community. I wanted to determine more effective ways to lure patrons to use the library's facilities. The club determined that we need to capitalize on the positive word of mouth that we'd received by having a sale. Offering Penn State T-shirts at a low price to anyone who used the library was our club's first largely successful sale. Instead of just coming in to put books on reserve, professors and faculty members were filing in throughout the day and asking how they could get a hold of these T-shirts. Naturally, students found the T-shirt sale to be great because the shirts were being sold at a lower price than in the campus bookstore.

The success of the shirt sale led to an on-campus car wash that offered another service to the campus and community. Mari understood that commuters, like me, brought their car to campus every day. The LSAB gave commuters a free car wash, with donations encouraged to support the club. Other club members and I hung around for four hours washing cars for students and faculty. The car wash proved to be a great way to spread awareness about our club and effective in giving us a solid reputation as a service organization.

The Ciletti Memorial Library's tenth anniversary happened to be in April of 2005. This meant that a lot of important people from various Penn State campuses would be gathering to commemorate this event. Mari and I began to work overtime to prepare for the anniversary. Mari knew that the LSAB had to make a strong

Patrick Troutman, speaking at the tenth anniversary of the Ciletti Memorial Library.

impression on the visitors from Penn State. I knew that this would be my last major event as the club's president and I wanted to leave my own impression.

On the afternoon of the commemoration ceremony, I stood before all of the representatives of Penn State as a sophomore on the verge of heading to Penn State–University Park. I had been asked to make a speech to give my input on what the library meant to me. In it, I praised Mari for her commanding expertise in guiding the LSAB to success. I also made sure to single out each of the library's employees for being incredibly friendly and helpful in getting me where I was. While Ann was not there to lend her reassuring smile, her warmth that attracted me to the library was very much intact.

With the ushering in of a newly elected president, I was no longer in charge of the club's decisions. Still, I continue to be informed about its latest success stories and hope to offer advice to the club until Mari decides that she is tired of me — which might never happen. The social and public speaking skills that I learned from working with the LSAB are greater than anything I've learned in my college career. In the Ciletti Memorial Library, I found more than a job and more than an education. I found a home.

As I departed Penn State–Schuylkill to pursue my degree in English, I knew that I was leaving the LSAB in good hands. I also knew that, wherever I went in life, I would be welcome back any time.

Ashley Fehr (left), Greg Bilotto, Loni Picarella and Patrick Troutman passing out programs and greeting guests at the Ciletti Memorial Library's tenth anniversary celebration.

What to Expect At Your First Meeting

Remember that most students have little or no time for extracurricular meetings because they are overwhelmed with classes, homework, study groups, athletic practice, music or theater group rehearsals, other clubs and jobs. We plan our library meetings for noon (a "common hour" that doesn't conflict with classes designated for such activities) and, when necessary, switch the day of the meeting to try to accommodate everyone's schedule. However, keeping a regular meeting time does help improve attendance.

I, Marianne, send out countdown e-mails beginning a few days ahead of time to remind students of the meeting and alert them that we will be serving lunch. When I see club members in the library, I remind them of the upcoming meeting. I also find out who might not be attending and let them know that they can meet with me at a later time and I will update them on the happenings. I have students who may have a make-up test or another commitment and just can't make it on the day of the meeting. These students stop by later in the afternoon or the next day and I let them know what is coming up next on the agenda for our club and hand them a

Library Student Advisory Board officers: Patrick Troutman (left), president; Loni Picarella, vice president; Greg Bilotto, treasurer; and Melissa Bautista, secretary.

copy of our minutes. After briefly discussing the topics that were on the meeting's agenda, it is likely that the student will have his or her own suggestions to share, or offer to dedicate their time to a special project.

This may take a little more of your time, but the students really appreciate that you take the time to meet with them one-on-one. This shows them that they really are a valued member of the club. Remember that even if a student can't attend all the meetings they can still contribute. We have had many students over the years who were in multiple clubs or had study groups at the same time as our meetings. Despite their conflicts, these students were still excellent members because they took the time to become informed about what they missed and contributed what they could. Even though the meeting times conflicted with other activities, they still had free time on other days to work on the display case, participate in fund-raisers, or make flyers and posters at home.

Our meetings typically last an hour, but could often go longer. Since we meet at noon we often provide food and encourage students to grab something to eat when they arrive, then get down to work. When I send out reminders, I try to get members to RSVP so we have an idea of how much food we will need to prepare. But once the precedent is set, be prepared for students to ask you if you will be serving food when you don't mention it in your meeting reminders. Also, be prepared for hungry students to be quite persuasive when trying to convince you to feed them. Some students also volunteer to contribute homemade cookies and pies for the meeting. By serving food you are not just luring students into your meeting, but also recognizing that they have busy schedules and competing demands for their time. Just be sure to check campus policies about serving food at your meetings.

Student Reflection on the Library Student Advisory Board and Club Meetings

Hannah Tracy reflects on her excitement about discovering a library club on campus, her experience with the LSAB, and what she will miss most about her membership in it. During her four semesters at Penn State Schuylkill Hannah served as club treasurer during the spring 2007 semester and LSAB president the following fall. Her diverse interests lead the group in new directions — such as having the library club host a salsa dance. Hannah is majoring in history and transferred to the Penn State University Park campus in the spring of 2008 to complete her degree.

Reflections on the Library Student Advisory Board
by Hannah Tracy

When I first was accepted to Penn State Schuylkill I got online and started looking at the Web site that listed all the different clubs and activities. I was really impressed that such a small campus had so many different kinds of clubs, but the one that really caught my eye was the Library Student Advisory Board. I had never heard of a library club before and it went straight to the top of my list for clubs I wanted to be part of when I came to Schuylkill. Now, after three semesters, it is going to be the club I miss the most when I leave. The LSAB is one of the most diverse clubs on campus in terms of its membership and activities. It is full of students who want to improve not just the library but the whole campus. For me, the library club became the club; whether it is community service or something like a salsa dance, everyone is always willing and excited to get involved. One of the things that I enjoyed the most about the club were the meetings themselves. This is where we come up with new ideas for what we want to do and get updates on projects we are already working on. Then, once the official meeting is over, you get to just eat good food and catch up with everyone. I have been in many different clubs while at Schuylkill, however the LSAB is the one that I have gotten the most out of and am most proud to have been a part of.

What Shall I Serve?

Everyone knows the way to a man's heart is through his stomach. Well, it's also true of college students, both male and female. As you may already know, a sure way to get students to show up at any event is to serve food. College students will eat just about anything that they can get for free. Many are away from home for the first time and are still adjusting to not having their parents' kitchen cabinets and refrigerator close at hand, or their parents' wallets for a pizza or a burger and fries. This need to fend for themselves can really make students' stomachs growl. I have seen students apparently live on bottles of Mountain Dew or energy drinks, tiny bags of chips or pretzels, and candy bars from the vending machines. When you announce that you will be serving lunch at your meeting, you tend to attract quite a few hungry students. Once you have them in your grasp, you have the opportunity to open their eyes to your club's mission and entice them to return.

The library staff typically provides lunch for the club members. Everyone provides something different so the burden does not fall on one person. Our typical menu items are simple to prepare: hot dogs, barbeque sandwiches or sloppy joes, chips and pretzels, drinks, fruit and dessert. If food prepared at home is not allowed at club meeting, perhaps you can offer quick and easy prepackaged foods as an alternative. Try sandwich meats and cheeses, jars of peanut butter and jelly and a couple loaves of bread for make-your-own sandwiches. And piping hot pizza is always just a phone call away. Staff members providing the lunch also enjoy having a hot, homemade alternative to typical lukewarm lunch fare. Because our club is active and there is a lot of pressure to be involved in club activities, we do not often find that students come just for the food — so we don't worry too much about having to feed the masses.

Another fun idea is to have theme lunches when a meeting falls near a holiday, or just for a pick-me-up during a stressful time of the semester. At Christmas we try to plan our meeting close to the holiday (and the end of the semester) and make the food festive with Christmas cookies, candy canes and little holiday gift bags with chocolate. We even play Christmas music in the background. (Adjust accordingly for the religious beliefs of your members and in accordance with campus policy.) On Halloween, some of the staff members dress in costumes and we hand out candy to all the students, staff, and faculty who come into the library. And at Thanksgiving, we make our favorite pumpkin cookies and decorate the library with miniature pumpkins, gourds, and dry corn. Use your imagination. You and your staff will have fun with this and start to look forward to the holiday seasons. Remember that your students are away from home, some of them for the first time; adjusting can be difficult for them. Involve club members by asking them to help with the decorations, picking out seasonal music for the meeting or an event, or stuffing little mugs with candies when you host these little celebrations. It makes them feel a little less homesick. Many times my club members have said to me how they truly appreciate the decorations, homemade cookies, and little gift bags.

Another way to make students a part of your campus community is to celebrate the birthdays of your members. Make or purchase cupcakes or a small birthday cake, and have your students decorate the meeting room with a "Happy Birthday" banner and balloons. If your club is small, you can do something special for each student. If individual celebrations on or near the day are too much, try recognizing members with recent birthdays at your monthly meetings. Have club members sign individual cards for any members celebrating their birthday that month, or use e-mail or Facebook to encourage members to send birthday wishes. Your students will be impressed.

Icebreakers

Your first meeting is the hardest and it can be very intimidating for both you and your students. You will probably have many students that do not know each other and as advisor you have to make them feel comfortable and help get them acquainted with each other. There are icebreakers for all kinds of meetings and gatherings. Some icebreakers help you learn names, and others help you to learn more about the individuals in your group. When we had our first meeting, we used an icebreaker remembered from a long-ago Tupperware party. There are many different books and Web sites that can help you find icebreakers that make introductions fun. See the recommended reading list at the end of this chapter for a few suggestions.

Icebreakers are a positive way of getting to know each other. They help get staff and students to relax around each other and can help students develop their social skills. They break the inevitable tension of being in a group of strangers and are a motivational way to start your first meeting. When doing these introductions, start with yourself and the library staff members. This helps the students relax a minute, gives them some time to consider what they would like to say, and lets them know a little bit about you before they share personal information about themselves.

We use different icebreakers every time we introduce a new student and find club members enjoy this amusing way of getting to know each other. To get started, have the students tell a little bit about themselves and what some of their interests are. Ask them what their majors are or what field they are interested in working in. If you frequently do icebreakers throughout the year, vary them so old members continue to learn new things about each other. Ask veteran members to share something new each time.

Some of the fun icebreakers we have tried are to have your students mention something they have done that they do not think anyone else has done. If another club member has already done it, the student has to keep trying until they find something that no one else has done. This is really fun and great way of getting to know everyone.

For a more physical icebreaker to get everyone warmed up, try using a balloon! Have your students stand in a circle. Everyone says his or her first name once. Then, throw the balloon in the circle and say someone's name. That person must run in and catch the balloon. Then that person has to remember and call out someone else's name and throw it back up in the air. Make sure everyone's name gets mentioned. This exercise is a great way to learn everyone's name and balloons are great because they can't break anything.

You will always have the quiet and shy students, as well as the more boisterous students who do not care where they are and what they say. You have to look around you and make sure that everyone gets a chance to speak. You can sometimes read faces and see when a shy student has an idea or a thought but is afraid to jump in. This is when you step in and say, "Do you have something you would like to share with us?" You will appreciate the students who can keep the conversations flowing, but remember to keep an eye out for the quiet students and give them an opportunity to step in and speak. Usually you will find that all the quiet students need is a little encouragement from you and they will be more comfortable with opening up and speaking at meetings. Everyone has to feel relaxed and have fun, or they might become uncertain about returning. As your meetings progress your club members will not hesitate to jump in and join the conversations because they will feel at ease with each other. Remember when you have new students join your club to make sure that everyone makes them feel welcome and wanted. When I recruit a new student I always send out an e-mail to all the club members, welcoming the new member to our club, and when they come to their first meeting I make sure that everyone introduces themselves before the start of the meeting to make the new member feel like they belong.

Icebreakers are also the perfect opportunity for the advisor to start learning the interests of the club's members. In the previous chapter we discussed the importance of finding out students' talents and interests in order to both make use of skills they bring to the club and help make the club's activities more relevant to students' interests. Keeping the club relevant keeps members active, and you might be surprised by some of the unique talents among your members. So, during those icebreakers, remember to jot down all the things you learn about the individuals in your club. See chapter 6 for more about the importance of getting to know your students.

Get Ready for Elections

At our first meeting we had to elect officers for the first time. Since I, Marianne, had never run a club and wasn't sure of all the rules at the beginning, we just played it by ear. First I asked my small group of members if anyone was interested in a position. Of course nobody raised their hands. "Come on guys, we need to have officers," I exclaimed. Finally I had four students grudgingly raise their hands. "Okay guys, who wants to do what?" Again, nobody answered me. They didn't really want the job, so they didn't care what they did. So I wrote the offices on little sheets of paper — president, vice-president, treasurer and secretary — and put them in a bowl. I made each one pick a paper and that was the job that they were going to do. This is *not* how you have real elections, but believe it or not it worked out well for us. The students who volunteered for the positions did a fantastic job in the positions they picked. The kids really took their jobs seriously and we had a remarkable year.

Every college club will have different rules and regulations for the election of officers. In our club, the constitution states that officers will be elected the first week of April and that all active members will have voting rights, except for the organization president and advisor. An active member is one who has attended a majority of events and meetings. The constitution also lists what each officer's job entails. Now, before we start elections, I make sure that the president reads aloud the constitution so that anyone interested in a certain position is reminded what is expected of them before nominating themselves or agreeing to run for an officer position. I also make sure that every member has a folder containing a copy of the constitution, a calendar of events, and a bookmark with the library hours and phone number.

Now that our club has grown in size and popularity, students vying for office have made the election process much more interesting. We usually need at least one or two new officers every year because of our high student turnover rate. Because we only have one meeting a month we start talking about elections early. I start in February by letting the members know how many officers we will need and what the job entails to find out who is interested in running for office. Once we have the names of students interested in an office position they are reminded of what the position's responsibilities are. The president reads over the constitution and reminds everyone of what each officer's position demands. We then have the interested students get up and speak to the club members to let them know why they are interested in this position and what they feel they can bring to the club. After the speeches conclude, the students leave the room and the eligible club members take a vote. You can do this either by a show of hands or written ballot. That choice is one your club could vote on, giving them an opportunity to express which they would feel most comfortable doing. When new officers are voted into office, they will typically take their seat in the following fall semester. This gives the student a chance to work with the current officer and to learn firsthand what their job requires before the end of the spring semester. After elections are over, I make sure to update the club's Web site and notify student affairs of the election results. I keep all the officers' names and their office position on the Web site under the heading of LSAB Officers, Past and Present. This is a great way to acknowledge all the hard work of your officers.

Recommended Reading

Barksdale, Ken, and Charles C. Hay III. "Friendly Development: Organizing and Using a Friends Group in Academic Library Development." *Kentucky Libraries* 61 (1997): 16–23.
    Discusses origins and accomplishments of a traditional academic library friends group at Eastern Kentucky University.

Bolton, Judy. "Twenty-eight Years as Friends." *Mississippi Libraries* 55 (Spring 1981): 10–12.
    Details the accomplishments of the traditional academic library friends group at Louisiana State University.

Bryans, Nancy R. "Library Volunteers Can Make a Difference." *Colorado Libraries* 25, no. 1 (Spring 1999): 42.
    Briefly details the accomplishments of the Women's Library Association of the University of Denver.

Clark, Charlene K. "Getting Started with Annual Funds in Academic Libraries." *Journal of Library Administration* 12, no. 4 (1990): 73–87.
    Discusses using traditional academic library friends groups to bolster your library's capital campaign.

Collins, Rowland Lee. "Friendship and Greatness." *CLIC Quarterly* 3 (December 1984): 22–25.

Well-written, inspirational essay on the nature of library friends groups, written at the passing of the Friends of the University of Rochester's tenth anniversary. Also includes notes on the accomplishments of this friends group.

Corson-Finnerty, Adam, and Laura Blanchard. "Using the Web to Find Old Friends and E-Friends." *American Libraries* 29, no. 4 (April 1998): 90–91.

Briefly describes the e-friend option at the University of Pennsylvania. While there is a membership fee to become a traditional friend of the University of Pennsylvania Libraries, becoming an e-friend is free and just a click away. The library hopes to expand their friend base through this program. A benefit of joining is regular updates on library activities.

Dolnick, Sandy. *Friends of Libraries Sourcebook.* Chicago: American Library Association, 1996.

Key source from the number one expert for those wanting to start a traditional friends of the library group, typically composed of community members, faculty, and alumni, to do large-scale fund-raising and advocacy work. Those interested in starting a nontraditional friends group may still find chapters on advocacy, event planning, and fund-raising quite useful.

Ferguson, Daniel. "Friends of the Library Groups: Implications for Promotion of Library Interests." *Australian Library Journal* 40 (November 1991): 328–335.

Provides a brief history of Australian and American library friends groups. The author asserts that while American friends groups have flourished since their inception in 1922, Australian friends groups have been slower to develop. Both public and academic library friends groups are discussed, including reference to the first academic library friends group, University Friends, conceived at Harvard University in 1925.

Haeuser, Michael. "Promoting Innovative Management and Services." *College & Research Libraries News* 49, no. 7 (July/August 1988): 419–422.

In the "Friends in Texas" section, the author briefly describes the formation and accomplishments of the Friends of the University of Texas at Arlington group. Library administration and staff were the recipients of a 1988 John Cotton Dana Special Award for Library Public Relations.

Haeuser, Michael. "What Friends Are For: Gaining Financial Independence." *Wilson Library Bulletin* 60, no. 9 (May 1986): 25–27.

Details the success of the Gustavus Library Associates, at Gustavus Adolphus College in St. Peter, Minnesota, at establishing an endowment for library collection purchases. Includes suggestions for the "conditions of success" for a friends group with the goal of large-scale fund-raising.

Hoadley, Irene B. "Future Perfect: The Library and Its Friends." *Library Administration & Management* 8, no. 3 (Summer 1994): 161–165.

Details the accomplishments of the traditional friends group at Texas A&M, including its contribution to the university's capital campaign.

Hopkins, James. "The Friends of the Air Force Academy Library: Friends in Deed!" *Colorado Libraries* 20 (Spring 1994): 37–39.

Details the accomplishments of the traditional friends group at the Air Force Academy Library.

"Icebreakers, Warmups, Energizers, & Deinhibitizers." Wilderdom.com, http://wilderdom.com/games/Icebreakers.html (accessed June 4, 2008).

Still more ice-breaker ideas, from balloon activities and "group juggling" to team-building exercises.

Linscome, Mary L. "Friends of the Libraries Reach Out." *Colorado Libraries* 26, no. 3 (2000): 6–8.

Details the organization and accomplishments of the traditional friends group at the University of North Colorado at Greeley. Many activities of this group are similar to those of Penn State Schuylkill's Library Student Advisory Board, though the group is not made up of university students.

Magnan, Robert. *147 Practical Tips for Using Icebreakers with College Students.* Madison, WI: Atwood, 2005.

Ice-breaker ideas to kick-start club meetings.

Munch, Janet Butler. "College Library Friends Groups in New York, New Jersey, and Connecticut." *College & Research Libraries* 49, no. 5 (September 1988): 442–447.

The report of a study of academic library friends groups at nondoctorate-granting colleges and universities in the tristate area of New York, New Jersey and Connecticut. One of the conclusions: "The real test of the Friends group ... is the leadership and the need to have one enthusiastic person willing to translate vision into reality."

Rea, Barbara S. "The Evolution of a Friends Group: Washington University Libraries' Bookmark Society." *Show-Me Libraries* 36 (September 1985): 19–23.

The friends group at the University of Washington (St. Louis, Missouri) found success when they changed their focus from fund-raising to literacy, attracting members of the community to join.

Sartori, Eve. "Friends of the Libraries, University of Nebraska-Lincoln." *Nebraska Library Association Quarterly* 23 (Summer 1992): 24–26.

Reviews the accomplishments of the traditional academic library friends group at the University of Nebraska-Lincoln.

Smyth, Elaine B., and Robert S. Martin. "Working with Friends of the Library to Augment Staff Resources: A Case History." *Rare Books & Manuscripts Librarianship* 9, no. 1 (1994): 19–28.
Details efforts of the traditional friends group at Louisiana State University to establish a graduate assistantship endowment.

Straw, John B. "Friends Make a Difference." *Indiana Libraries* 25, no. 3 (2006): 13–15.
Details the accomplishments of the traditional academic library friends group at the Ball State University Bracken Library.

Taylor, Merrily E. "It's Hard to Make New Friends: What to Think About in Creating a Friends of the Library Group." *Library Trends* 48, no. 3 (Winter 2000): 597–605.
Discusses points to consider when thinking about starting a traditional academic library group as a new source of library support.

West, Edie. *The Big Book of Icebreakers: 50 Quick, Fun Activities for Energizing Meetings and Workshops.* New York: McGraw-Hill, 1999.
More ice-breaker ideas to kick-start club meetings.

5

Understand and Interpret
Policies and Procedures

Every college and university will have unique policies regulating student organizations and standard procedures or protocol for conducting club business. For these reasons, we will not go into a lot of detail about specific policies and procedures here. Instead, in this chapter we will highlight a few important areas in which we recommend making a point to learn your college or university's policies and procedures. These include finding an appropriate meeting time, holding club elections, annual reporting to student affairs and your library, ensuring student safety at club events, necessity of making contracts when working with outside vendors, and insurance requirements. Here we will use examples of situations we encountered and the corresponding policies and procedures from our institution that helped guide us through the process.

As a constant in the group from one year to the next, the advisor plays an important role in the club. Part of this role is to help students understand, interpret, and adhere to the policies and procedures pertaining to student clubs at your university. Some of these policies and procedures may require the advisor to submit or oversee the submission of documents, such as applications and annual reports. Keeping good records makes these tasks much easier, and will contribute to your club's success. With this in mind, we will discuss the types of records you may need to keep and will share tips on how to keep good records.

Policies and Procedures Unique to Your Institution

Policies and procedures will vary from one institution to the next. Some may have strict rules that club members must follow to maintain their organization's status and funding. Others may be much less rigid. Perhaps this will depend on the size of your university, the scope of the clubs under these rules, and the history of student clubs (and their history of causing trouble) at your university. However, do not let this discussion of policies and procedures deter you from being involved with a student club. With a bit of effort to stay on top of any changes to the rules and some good, efficient record keeping, adhering to the established policies and procedures is not difficult. As always, a good relationship with the staff in your student affairs department helps your club stay on the straight and narrow path to success.

As a representative of the university and a common thread in the club from one year to the next, it is typically the advisor whose role is to help members and club leaders understand and adhere to your university's policies and procedures relating to university clubs. In this section you will read about some of the key areas in which to discover and understand the rules of your institution.

Meeting Times

To encourage students to participate in extracurricular activities, universities may designate times during which clubs *may* meet, or simply establish a regular block of time during which they *may not* meet. Policies about club meeting times also prevent students from feeling that they have to choose between attending class and becoming involved on campus. Our campus has a "common hour" during which clubs are encouraged to hold their meetings. This is good because no classes meet during this time, with the exception of a few long science-lab classes. However, there is a lot of competition for students' attention during the common hour. We try to remain flexible, catching up students who choose other obligations or split their time between the two meetings, either over the course of the hour or by going to one meeting one month and the other meeting the next month. We also have to compete with a very important element of everyone's day: lunch. We have taken this negative and used it to our advantage. Feeding them is one way we have been able to encourage students to become involved and stay involved with the Library Student Advisory Board.

In a typical situation, the club's advisor may not be required, or even necessarily encouraged to attend club meetings. Indeed, the student club literature for our university suggests that student club leaders invite the advisor to club meetings as a way to reach out and improve the club's relationship with the advisor. However, for a club such as this — where students are advising a campus institution and the club advisor may be acting as liaison between the club and the library's administration — having the advisor regularly attending club meetings is a necessity. When considering who will play the role of club advisor and liaison from the library, also take your institution's policies or guidelines regarding meeting times into consideration. For example, some organizations may require or encourage club meetings be held in the evenings. Will this person be able to attend all or most meetings during the prescribed time?

Finally, if your club chooses to hold its meeting outside the prescribed time, consider the consequences. You will likely have more classes competing against your selected time slot than you would clubs and other activities during the lunch or common hour. This could mean fewer students involved with your club, and perhaps lead to some exclusivity. It could also be acting counter to the university's primary mission of educating students.

Holding Elections

To ensure that all elections are fair and that there will be leaders in each group who will keep the club active, your university or student government may have policies and procedures for holding elections. The university or student government will want accurate records of all student leader changes, as important information is often disseminated to student clubs through the club leaders.

The role of the club advisor in elections may be minimal. In our case, it is the responsibility of the club president to conduct the elections, so the advisor helps the student understand how elections are conducted and ensures that the name and contact information for newly elected leaders is forwarded to our student affairs department. The advisor also reminds students a few months in advance that elections are coming up and encourages them to begin thinking about running for office. These students are the potential leaders the advisor will be working with closely the next year. So, take a look at who would make good club leaders, pull these select few aside sometime, and encourage them to take on the challenge. Encouraging students to accept a new leadership role is the first step in helping them further develop their leadership skills.

Advisor interest in the election process helps ensure the continuity of the club. Members who perceive weak leadership may lose interest in the club; others may be inspired to run for office to do something about it. Leaders with little interest in finding their replacement could lead the club to its end, especially with an apathetic membership. Reminding current leaders about their responsibilities, the election process, and any upcoming deadlines for holding elections helps ensure the elections are held fairly and in a timely manner. In our case, starting the process early helped build competition for the posts and encouraged those running for election to seriously think about the direction in which they would like to take the club under their leadership and what directions other members wanted to take, and even to do a little bit of campaigning. In our case this has only been in good fun and hasn't turned nasty.

Annual Reporting

Formal annual reports are not a required condition of club status at our university, but our student affairs department does request the courtesy of an annual report of activities. These reports help student affairs determine the health of student organizations on campus and they also serve to keep the staff abreast of the activities and interests of groups. This allows them to match clubs with possible funding opportunities or pair them with other groups with similar interests to achieve a common goal. For these reasons, annual reports may be required at your college or university.

Our student affairs department is largely interested in the numbers — a snapshot of how club funds were spent and membership numbers, including the year's gains and losses in membership. The club's advisor and student leaders should work together to compile this report using the records you have collected throughout the year, including meeting minutes, lists of items purchased for donation, attendance at special events, and the club's budget ledger. Whether required or not, you will likely find that members of your library administration will also be quite interested in reviewing this capsule of club activity, perhaps even working it into internal documents of the library's outreach activities. Club members will also like having this reminder of the projects they worked on throughout the year, perhaps even to demonstrate their talents on a resume or job application. The student affairs department may want these reports, or something similar, out of interest in keeping student activity programs healthy. Inactive groups may need to be disbanded, or need a new advisor to get them back on track.

Student Safety at Club Events

Be sure you understand policies and guidelines regarding any activities that might put a student's safety at risk. This includes unforeseen events on bus trips, food served at club meetings or special events, or even accidents while doing fund-raising. Student safety — and university liability — are important concerns for any university, making them important concerns for you. There are often policies regarding environmental health and safety issues, as well as general safety considerations for events. You may have the option or be required to use standard university waivers and releases for university sponsored events both on- and off-campus — so there is no need to reinvent the wheel when it comes to safety. Consult with student affairs, or the appropriate office at your campus, for detailed information and make safety a routine part of all event-planning activities.

Contracts

Be familiar with policies and guidelines regarding off-campus food service and outside services for hire. While some caterers and performers may be satisfied with a verbal agreement and your acceptance of their cancellation policy, a signed contract protects the interests of the club and the university, as well as the service provider. A standard contract ensures the service is delivered as outlined in the contract, with legal grounds for seeking restitution if not. It also ensures payment to the provider for services delivered.

But don't let talk of contracts discourage you from hiring outside catering or entertainment. As with safety waivers and release forms, it is likely there are boilerplate contract templates for you to use, and plenty of people on campus — perhaps even coworkers — to help you through the process the first few times. Our campus student affairs department made a contract on behalf of the club with the salsa band for the salsa dance — an event requiring much advance planning on behalf of both the club and the band. But no contract was needed for our fund-raisers because the items were purchased with club funds up front, with a typical product-return policy protecting us if the goods received were not as ordered. As you would expect with a fund-raiser, items were then sold for a small profit to recoup our investment and raise a little extra for the club's fund.

Insurance

There may also be certain events for which you will need insurance. This might sound scary, or even unnecessary. But, despite your best intentions and watchful eye, events such as rock climbing, fireworks, or even henna tattoos and illusionists may require proper liability insurance. This protects both the club and participants in the event of an accident.

Important details such as this are why we continually recommend having a great working relationship with the staff in your student affairs department. Typically, the staff there can quickly tell you when insurance will be needed and how to obtain it. Ask as many questions as you need to until you understand the policies at your institution. This is a great example of why it is important to attend informational meetings held by your student affairs department — the more knowledge you obtain, the greater your club can become.

Your Responsibilities as Advisor

Members and club leaders come and go. This keeps the club fresh and is a necessary part of life on a college campus. But ideally the individual playing the role of advisor to the club is a constant. As a constant in the group, the advisor should understand the university's policies and procedures in order to help students understand and adhere to them. The advisor can be considered an official representative of the university, and, as a university representative and a mature adult, any club advisor should recognize the importance of adhering to university policies and procedures. Some of these policies and procedures may require the advisor to submit or oversee the submission of documents such as applications and annual reports, making record keeping a necessary part of the club's activities. In this section we will discuss the importance of helping students understand your college or university's policies and procedures, as well as offer suggestions for the types of records to keep at your fingertips that will make the above tasks much easier.

Help Students Understand Policies and Procedures

As one of the few constants in the club from one year to the next, it is not only important for the club advisor to know the rules, but also to always be aware of any changes. Our student affairs department occasionally holds budget and policy meetings for club leaders. When attending these meetings, be sure to collect samples of new forms and informational handouts to update your files. These will reflect changes to important policies and procedures that must be followed by your club. In our case, they are often revised and updated from one year to the next, so keeping up to date will be a regular, but simple task if you keep your notes and files organized.

It is also important for the club advisor to have a thorough understanding of the policies and procedures in order to help students understand and adhere to them. When you get your student officers together for the first time it is very important to go over the university's policies and procedures for managing club meetings. While talking with them, make a point of reminding club leaders of their responsibilities, as established in the club's constitution. Also discuss any university policies or procedures important to their role in the club. Explain that following these procedures will help them perform their job duties to the best of their abilities. For example, the president needs to be aware of procedures for conducting an officer election, the secretary should be aware of any procedures for recording minutes or submitting reports to student affairs, and the treasurer needs to be aware of policies and procedures pertaining to the management of the club's funds. Though the rules and the necessary paper trail might seem to make a simple task overly complex or impede the progress of the club, these rules exist for a reason — typically to protect the safety of the students or the interests of the university. Helping students understand this can make their adherence to the rules a little easier.

In one example from our experience, a new campus policy prohibited us from repeating a successful fund-raiser. In our first year the Library Student Advisory Board decided to sell decorative candles. This was a very successful fund-raiser — the candles made dorms and apartments seem a little more homey, added some ambiance, and perhaps masked the smells associated with four people living in a small space. Given the success in the previous year, some of the club members wanted to do this fund-raiser again the second year. However, the campus policy had changed and candles were now prohibited on campus. Consequently, the selling of candles was also banned. The club members were disappointed in this, but after explaining that the university had taken such a stand to protect the safety of the students they agreed with the importance of having such a policy to prevent fires on campus and settled on a different fund-raiser.

In another case, the LSAB applied for money to procure a salsa band for a dance on campus. The club was granted the money to host this event, but leaders were told that they would not be able to use this event as a fund-raiser. Once the university began to regularly collect a student activities fee and allot funds to clubs to finance such out-of-class activities, the new policy prevented groups from charging for events funded by the money collected from the student activities fee. In other words, you do not want to charge the students a second time for something they have already paid for. When put in these terms, the club members understood and decided to still put their energies into planning the dance, and hope to plan others in the future. These dances are a good way to have fun, meet new students, introduce them to the work of the club, and entice them to join. To tie the library into these events, club members create fantastic displays based on the theme of the dances by using items from the library's collections.

Keeping Good Records

Keeping good club records contributes to the group's success as a club. Important documents such as meeting minutes, budget records and annual reports kept on file with the advisor or the student affairs office provide a club history for future club leaders to review. And keeping the current year's documents on file at the library with the club's advisor makes important information easily accessible for completing applications and the group's annual report. In this section we will offer tips on keeping good records and the types of records you may need to keep.

- PART OF YOUR SUCCESS AS A CLUB

Once your club is established you will have quite a bit of paperwork, including money allocation forms, insurance forms, vendor forms, membership lists, and club minutes. Keeping good records makes it much easier to get paperwork completed and submitted on time. It is imperative to attend any training sessions offered by your student affairs department on behalf of the student government or other body regulating student club policies at your institution. These training sessions will help you and your student leaders learn about policies your club must follow to remain active, help you understand the process for obtaining funds for the club, and explain responsible use of the money. Both you and your officers will need to keep updated on all the new rules and regulations. Between meetings your student affairs department may send new information needed to keep your club up and running successfully. These trainings and meetings have helped us tremendously. They have also given us good ideas and provided tips for advising the club leaders on how to govern meetings, running the club more efficiently, signing up new members, and helping build our pride in our club and university.

• Tips for Keeping Good Records

First and foremost, make sure you work closely with all of your officers to maintain records. Discuss with them the types of records they need to keep copies of for the club's files and show them where to file them. Discussing expectations in advance keeps the advisor from having to hound leaders for the information, although this may still be necessary sometimes.

Planning for meetings and special events will go more smoothly if room arrangements are made as far in advance as possible. Room arrangements include room reservations, as well as furniture and equipment requests. Ideally, your club will want to meet in the same place each week to keep the schedule simple for everyone. Try to make room arrangements for the following year *before* your group's final meeting in the spring semester. This way you can share the new schedule with returning members and secure a great location. Double-check on your arrangements a few weeks before the meeting or event and have copies of your room requests nearby in case problems arise.

Next, it is essential to keep first-class financial records. Whether the club's advisor or treasurer is responsible for club funds (depending on the policies of your institution), keep a ledger book tracking club funds and train your treasurer how to use it, how to make deposits and withdrawals, and how to record these transactions in the ledger. Also make sure all club leaders are aware of the importance of having itemized receipts for purchases and what needs to be done with them. If original receipts need to be submitted to a budget office, train your leaders to keep a legible photocopy of the receipt on file. Work vigilantly with your treasurer to ensure that club funds are properly handled. It is likely that you, as advisor, will need to sign for monies spent, making you ultimately responsible for the club's budget.

Also track all funds allotted to the club. This can vary by institution, but your club may have both restricted and unrestricted funds. Restricted funds are the monies provided by the student government or the school's student activity fee to purchase specific items, approved in advance. Typically the funding for these items will be requested and approved at the beginning of each semester. Your unrestricted balances are the monies you, as a club, have collected from your fund-raisers and any outside grants. As the name implies, you can spend these monies any way your club deems appropriate, or let the money build up in the account over a few years for a big purchase. Finally, have your treasurer read off all balances to the membership at your monthly meetings so members know where the club stands financially. This way budget information is also recorded in the meeting minutes.

It is important to take attendance at each meeting. Have a sign-in sheet to collect the names and email address of members and visitors. This will allow you to track how your enrollment is advancing or declining from year to year. If you don't have time to speak with visitors about their interest in joining the club after the meeting, follow up with a friendly e-mail.

It is also essential to keep accurate meeting minutes. Typically, this will be done by the club's secretary. Take the time before your club's first meeting of the year to review with your secretary the types of things it is important to record in the minutes. You may also wish to give your secretary a sample of past minutes to show what to record and to use as a reference for formatting. Your student affairs department may also offer tips or training for students responsible for keeping their club's minutes. Ask your secretary to type up the minutes as soon as possible after the meeting and distribute them to the group. Keep a copy of each meeting's minutes in a readily accessible place. This will allow you to review discussions and decisions, verify dates, and will help immensely with your end-of-the-year report.

As advisor, I can be a stickler for taking thorough minutes because I constantly refer back to them throughout the year and even into the next year. Talk with your secretary to let him or her know what you expect and explain the importance of having this record of events. The basics for taking good minutes would be to format the minutes according to the agenda and include:

- date and time the meeting was called to order
- kind of meeting (regular or special)
- names of club members in attendance, noting any visitors or new members
- announcements from club advisor, library staff, student affairs department, or club members (such as dates of upcoming fund-raisers, special events, or trainings)
- for each item on the agenda, major discussion points and who made the point
- for each item on the agenda, any action that needs to be taken, members who will do the task, and date task needs to be completed
- for each item on the agenda, any items voted upon and how the membership voted, noting whether motion was approved or declined
- date, time, and location of next meeting.

Remind students to use the agenda as their guide for taking notes. Meeting minutes should record major discussion points, but does not need to be a transcript of the meeting.

All of these records may be used to create end-of-the-year reports. End-of-the-year reports may or may not be required by your sponsoring organization. Either way, reviewing your accomplishments from the past year will be a good investment of your time. A brief, one-page, end-of-the-year report allows you to quickly see what your club has accomplished and contributed to your library and campus community. At a glance, you can compare one year to the next and see what worked and what did not. This can also help with planning for the upcoming year. Having a summary report on hand can also help you promote the club and easily share your experience with others. From the meeting minutes, personal notes, and other records you can quickly compile a snapshot of funds received and see how the money was spent. Include lists of books, videos, equipment, supplies, and any other items purchased, as well as funds donated to worthy causes and other miscellaneous expenditures. Include total numbers of members gained at the beginning of the year and lost at the end due to turnover to help reflect the enormity of your groups' accomplishments in light of its losses and gains.

Our student affairs department keeps a file on all the clubs on campus, and requests that advisors send copies of all information about their clubs' activities during the year. We routinely send duplicate files that we keep on the club, such as updates on our member numbers, dates of club meetings, meeting agendas and minutes, notes about significant accomplishments, lists of purchases that were donated to the library, and monies donated to charity.

6

Goals and Objectives

Our Library Student Advisory Board only has one very broad goal, as stated in the club's constitution: promote student input and involvement in library services and programming. We don't have any written objectives or strategies for achieving this goal, but have identified a number of unwritten objectives. These include: improve the library as a student space by advising library administration on student needs and desires (improve student-centeredness); increase student usage of the library by sharing the value of the library with student peers and faculty; and enhance library collections with donations of materials of student choice. Secondary, unwritten goals might be improving student experience on campus by sponsoring special events, developing a sense of community on campus, and improving students' leadership skills. As you may see, our one, broad goal gives us a lot of flexibility to tailor the group to student interests, including charitable donations.

While it may seem that gift giving outside the library is counter to the mission of the club, it creates a positive profile of the group in the outside community. Although we do not currently have any intention of broadening the scope of the club, this could pave the way for a potential future goal of attracting outside community members to the group. Such a group would be similar to traditional friends of academic library groups. It would increase the club's fund-raising power, paving the path to a future collections endowment. We do not currently have any plans to take such an action, but this could be a goal of your student advisory board.

In order to achieve the overarching goals of the club and make the group a success, effort must be made each day to build relationships with club members and motivate them to contribute their best efforts to the success of the club. On the following pages we will offer guidance and tips on working day to day to make the group a success in order to achieve your group's goals and objectives. The chapter will conclude with some tips for planning for the future. We hope this is the chapter advisors will turn to when they need some advice on navigating their group out of rocky waters and back on the path to success.

The Advisor's Job

It is probably no surprise that lot of work goes into achieving the goals and objectives of a club like our Library Student Advisory Board. To make the group a success, the advisor needs to work a little each day on building relationships with club members and motivating them through difficult times. We have found that to consistently have a successful club from one year to the next, the activities for each year need to be tailored to the interests of the group. Make a point of getting to know your members and finding out their interests, but also let them know that they can come and talk with you. Students can get stressed out about schoolwork, as well as their family and social lives. Sometimes they just need a sympathetic ear and maybe to step back from the club for a few weeks. But you always need to motivate them to return when they are ready. And, sometimes you need a little motivation yourself. Dedicated club members can be a source of motivation. This is also a time when you can lean on colleagues for support.

With a solid foundation built by sturdy relationships with your club members, achieving the objectives of the club becomes much easier. When students know they are more than just a name on an attendance list or warm body at a meeting, when they know they are valued for their unique talents and the effort they put into the club, when they know they cannot just come for the free lunch and not contribute to the club, they work much harder to make the club successful. In the remainder of this chapter we will talk about strategies for building strong relationships with your student members and will conclude with things you need to know about finding out their library-related needs and desires, getting members to be effective library advocates, and fund-raising.

Develop Relationships

- BE AVAILABLE

    Letting students know that you are available is as easy as telling them you have an open-door policy. If you find you can't balance an open-door policy with your work, perhaps let them know what your office hours are instead. If they feel comfortable talking with you, they will come. Marianne has found that new students, away from home for the first time, have made the most use of her sympathetic ear. Concerns stemming from frustrations with course scheduling or issues with roommates can be resolved by guiding them to someone on campus who can help them resolve their problems. Picking up the phone and letting someone at another student service point know you are sending a student over for help can go a long way in establishing a good relationship with that individual. Sometimes students just need someone to listen, but once in a great while you might encounter a student in distress that needs professional assistance. Be aware of student counseling and health services on your campus. It never hurts to offer this information to a student. Your campus may even have a program in place for alerting counselors about students in distress so they can reach out to them if they don't come in for help. As discussed in the first chapter, all of this may contribute to the retention of students on campus, at least of the ones in your club.

• Find Out Club Members' Interests

Taking the time to learn a little about each of your members is a great way to begin the process of creating relationships with them. On a campus where new students may only know a few people, or are missing friends and family at home, this can make a real difference to them. The fact that you took the time to get to know them, and allowing them to get to know you, makes a powerful statement about the club's values. Ask your students about their likes and dislikes, their hobbies, what they did in high school or what they like to do in their spare time. You can do this at your meetings — especially the first meeting when you are getting to know each other — or any place you run into students on campus. You may even find students stop by your office or desk wanting to talk. They might have something on their mind, or maybe they just want to pass some time. Invite them in and have a nice discussion.

Make a note of each student's interests for your files — this information may come in handy later. Using this information you can tap certain students for special projects based on their interests, or even tailor projects according to their interests. As you build a closer relationship with your students you will find out even more about them. A lot of students are afraid to open up at the meetings, but when they are talking one-on-one with you they tend to express themselves more freely.

We had one student who was very shy and quiet. She went through a whole semester working in the library and as a member of the club, and never told any of us she had written and published a young adult novel. As soon as we found out about this we asked her if she would mind if we let all the club members know the exciting news and plan to have a book signing for her at the library. The event was well attended — yet another event drawing positive attention from students to the library. (See chapter 7, pages 126 & 127.)

We had another student who loves photography, and even had his own equipment. Our library keeps an archive of all campus faculty and staff accomplishments, including a photograph. At one of our meetings, the head librarian suggested the club could update the pictures in the archive. With today's digital photography, it is so easy to take the pictures from the camera, upload them onto your computer, and save them in a specially marked folder. From there you can archive by whatever means you choose — such as printing on high-quality photo paper, archiving on a networked

LSAB meeting in May 2007, being held in the Ciletti Library's Special Collections Room which houses books on local history, books by local authors and a collection of rare books.

server, or storing a backup copy of the photographs on a CD or DVD. The club members working on this project used one of the library's computers for all their work. This was convenient for the students because it gave them a dedicated space to work and was convenient for the library because the files were stored on one of our computers for easy access.

This project was a wonderful opportunity for all the students who liked photography, and setting up appointments to take photos was a great way for students to meet faculty and staff—and for them to be introduced to students as representatives of the library. This could be a great project for any library club. Having photographs taken of your campus, your faculty, and your staff is a wonderful way to keep campus archives up to date for future use. As a special occasion approaches (for example, a retirement, anniversary, or award ceremony), it is great to be able to go into the archive and easily retrieve old pictures and articles kept on file about that particular person or event. It also helps build the library's relationship with the faculty, staff, and administration. You will find that many of them are pleased to learn that the library is keeping a record of their significant accomplishments as part of the campus history.

Top: LSAB meeting in September 2007 in Ciletti Library's Studio. The club has grown so much that we needed to change our meeting room to accommodate our members. *Bottom*: LSAB's newest members posing in front of the Ciletti Memorial Library, Penn State Schuylkill, for the LSAB archives.

Most recently, the campus development office requested that club members create a special display of memorabilia for a scholarship fund-raising dinner in honor of a retired, yet still beloved music instructor, Professor James Beach. The fund-raising dinner was to honor Mr. Beach and his importance to our campus, as well as raise money for his scholarship fund. The event reunited former Schuylkill Chorale members and provided them with another opportunity to sing under the direction of their former leader.

The library's campus history archive holds many photographs and event programs, as well as the scrapbooks kept for many years by student members of the cam-

The Library Student Advisory Board created a special display of memorabilia for a scholarship fund-raiser dinner honoring Professor James Beach, retired music instructor at Penn State Schuylkill.

pus chorale group. Using these materials, club members with artistic skills and experience with scrapbooking were able to develop wonderful displays reviving twenty years' worth of memories for the diners. This is a fantastic way to remember someone's achievements. People stayed well past the end of the event to take it all in. So, while their efforts helped raise money for campus scholarships, they also helped increase the visibility of the club and its efforts in the campus and alumni communities. The beautiful displays also increased the visibility of the library and its archive among campus alumni. The things you and your club do today can affect what happens tomorrow. Alumni are a great asset when campaigning for support in the future.

Motivation: Staying Afloat

There will come a time when you have a semester or two where your club isn't on top of things like other years. You feel like you have to push and prod them just to do the simplest jobs. There are some days when you wonder if you even want to continue with the club, but don't lose hope. It can happen to the best of clubs — it has even happened with ours. We had one semester where nothing was getting accomplished. When you are frustrated and ready to give up, just get along as best as you can and try not to punish yourself or your students with unnecessary tasks. This is a time to consider your priorities and maybe even reconsider the direction of the club. Are your members detached from the group because they aren't interested in the club's activities? Or are they simply overburdened with schoolwork, out-of-class activities, family and personal-life issues, or forced to place a paying job as a higher priority than their volunteer club membership?

These are the pages you will turn to when you hit rough times with your club, when you need help motivating your students to keep up or increase their involvement with the group, or when you need help motivating yourself to continue working toward the goals you and the club have set for yourselves and the library. There will be semesters when your club will excel, when they will be at your side with ideas constantly, when they will hold successful fund-raisers, and when their efforts will make the club a huge success. Then there will be semesters when your members are just too busy or start to lose interest. This happens to all clubs and someday it may happen to yours.

- MOTIVATE YOURSELF

Some days, you just can't seem to find the motivation to continue. You feel tired and overworked. You need some inspiration. Former club members may be more than willing to help in this capacity. Without even really trying, I, Marianne, have found that I have forged such a bond with former club members that staying in touch with them was effortless. On more than one occasion I have contacted past presidents and asked for their help to keep me motivated when times were tough. Their encouraging words to me have never failed.

Past club officers and members can be a great inspiration to both new members and to you, as advisor. Keeping past officers and other interested members on your e-mail list keeps them updated on the progress of the club. Even though they are no longer official members and cannot vote, you may find they still like to be aware of the club's activities. They may even have ideas and advice for the new members. Their congratulatory e-mails when the club accomplishes something are also great motivators for you and the club. You will find that every year you have members who ask to stay in the loop and receive these e-mails. They still give suggestions and can be a boost to you, the advisor, when you have a semester or year when you feel like you are not accomplishing as much as other years.

When you work so closely with the club and its activities, sometimes you might overlook easy, innovative solutions to a problem. So step out of the box. Talk with friends and coworkers; ask them for any ideas that might help your club grow. Take all workshops that are offered for the clubs on your campus. These clubs talk and work together to improve the campus — you can learn so much from others. Focus on being creative. Make the club fun for you and your student members. You have to like what you do to prosper.

Finally, don't overlook your library's collections. Check out books on motivation. There are many books out there on the subject of motivating yourself and motivating students. For suggestions, check out the recommended reading list at the end of this chapter.

• MOTIVATE YOUR MEMBERS

Repeat this mantra: Stay positive. With persistence you will again reach that level of success you want. Then keep doing all the things you did to recruit your members and get them involved in the first place. Keep your e-mails and reminders going. Remember sometimes students aren't motivated because they don't understand your club's concepts. Club members who are unsure of the group's goals will seldom perform well. You will want to explain to your new club members what your club wants to accomplish and how it is trying to help students become more familiar with the library and be more at ease. Here are a few more suggestions to help you motivate your club members:

◁ Sit down with your student club members and have them write down or verbally share one thing that really interests them, whether gaming, poetry, dances, making friends, movies, photography, philanthropy, art, writing, or singing. If written, collect and have one person read these ideas out loud. As you go through them, discuss each answer and see how you as a club can incorporate these ideas into a special event, fund-raiser, humanitarian act, open house, library mixer, or field trip.

‹ Have contests and giveaways to motivate members. I have found that students love competition — and free stuff. It doesn't matter what they are competing for, they just love to compete. Turn your fund-raisers or projects into little competitions; have members work in teams to get projects done. For prizes, hand out mugs filled with candy, car magnets, or key chains with your school's emblem on them. Students also appreciate when you present them gift certificates to Subway, Burger King, or local pizza and sub shops.

‹ Invite your school's president or chancellor, student affairs director, or a library administrator to one of your luncheons. Ask them if they would give a brief motivational speech to your club members. We occasionally have speakers come and visit with us during one of our monthly get-togethers. The students really appreciate the time these speakers give and the speakers get to see the library club in action.

‹ Remember that you can only do so much with the club members you have. If your student membership is low, you don't want to overwhelm them with huge projects. Keep those larger projects for another time when you have enough students to work on them. Keep a notebook of the ideas that you and your club members would like to try in the future and go back and check on it from time to time. When you do have your membership numbers up and you have the help you need, then your club can work on those larger projects.

You may have to rely on yourself and others to take up the slack of the members, but it is usually only for a brief period of time and well worth it in the end. Even though your club may have its down times, remember to always offer encouragement and appreciation for their contributions. *Never* tell your club that they aren't doing as well as other years or that you're disappointed in them. *Always* make heartfelt comments showing your appreciation for the time they give to the club and thank them for making the effort to come to the meetings. Encourage, support, and give them the confidence they need, reassure them that every little thing that they do for the club is helpful. Build up your students with positive reinforcement.

Importance of Showing Your Appreciation

Always remember to thank your leaving officers and members for all the hard work they have done for your club. Let them know that you appreciate all their efforts and time. When any member leaves the club, we always have a round of applause and personally thank each and every one of them for all the hard work that they have done over their time with the club. Ask them if they want to remain on your e-mail list and if they still want to keep in touch about the club and its activities. Following are some ideas for showing club members your appreciation for all their hard work and dedication.

• A FEW WAYS TO SHOW YOUR APPRECIATION

Certificates of appreciation are easy to create and students like being recognized for their work. First, either purchase or create a certificate that you are happy with. Creation can be accomplished with any word processing program or other tools. Once you have the basic certificate established, you only have to change the name and date on each one. We purchase fine parchment paper on which to print the certificates; you can find this at any establishment that sells office supplies. These stores will have a variety of colors and consistencies you can choose from. Once you have the certificate printed you can just present them to your officers as is, or place them in a frame for added effect.

Depending on how much money your club has in its accounts, you can also give a souvenir or gift card along with the certificate. If the club funds are dwindling or such purchases are prohibited using the club's funds, try collecting donations from library staff members. When one or more of our officers are leaving we typically give them a Penn State key chain along with their award certificate.

We also take pictures of our leaving officers and club members. If you have a digital camera you can e-mail photos to club members for their own personal use. We like to print them out on photo paper and put everyone's name on the back for future reference. This is an easy and inexpensive way to show your gratitude to club members. We keep digital copies of these pictures in our club archives and print them for the victory log. Make sure to put the names and dates on all your pictures so that when you look back years from now, you will have all the information you need.

Here are a few more ideas for showing your appreciation to club members:

◄ Have a special luncheon for your departing members — throw a pizza party or have a picnic outside. Maybe bring a cake that is lettered "Thank you." Invite faculty and staff to give recognition to these hard-working individuals.

◄ Offer to give references to your club members. These students will be needing references for college work-study programs, internships, scholarships, and job applications. You have worked with these students and have witnessed their hard work and ambition. You know their work ethic and integrity. Let your students know that you will be happy to do this for them. Some may even be relieved to hear this coming from you, afraid to ask out of fear that it might be an imposition.

Discovering Student Needs and Desires

Now that we have covered the basics of building relationships and motivating both your club members and yourself, let's move on to the main objectives of the club. As demonstrated earlier in this book, it doesn't take much more than simply posing the question to them to find out what students would like to change about the library. However, it is also important to assure them that their suggestions will be taken seriously and to create an atmosphere where students feel comfortable talking with you.

First-meeting icebreakers and the advisor's steps toward building relationships with members will both contribute to increasing students' comfort levels. If at the first meeting you try to start a dialogue about steps that can be taken toward making the library more student-centered and you find that people aren't opening up, give them some time, move on, and try again later. New students in particular might need some time to explore the library first.

You will also need to discover what will work best for your group regarding the presence at club meetings of someone from library administration — or someone in the position to affect change. This can give students a sense of the group's importance and help them realize that their suggestions are being taken seriously, or it may make them quiet and uncomfortable during your club meeting. In this case, what might work better is to have a brainstorming session, then invite library leaders to the next meeting so club leaders can present well-formed ideas. Alternately, club leaders can arrange an appointment with library administrators to present their ideas and a plan for implementing them, starting a dialogue between these two parties. Regardless of how you convey club ideas to library administration, in the event that one of its suggestions cannot be implemented make sure that students know *why* they cannot. Otherwise, you risk losing their membership if people feel they aren't taken seriously and the library student advisory board is a waste of their time.

Coaching on the Value of the Library

Students will easily talk about what the club is working on, particularly when they are excited about it. They might bring it up the in the context of a class discussion, in a meeting with a professor, or simply a chance encounter with a friend or acquaintance. But what is most important here is that they are talking about the library club, and the library by association, with their friends. Our attempts to pass our excitement about the library on to the club members in large doses have largely been met with glassy-eyed stares. This is an objective of the club that we would like to expand upon, but it seems to work better in small doses — such as introducing students to the campus archive when they have been asked to work on a scholarship dinner project for the development office.

So, although we do not have club members out to promote library collections and services at every opportunity, they are representing the library through their work with other groups and special events on campus. This work has attracted new members to the club, giving the library administration an opportunity to market the library to new students. And perhaps we are best suited for that role. The popular movies and best-selling novels have attracted a lot of students to the library, giving us a chance to show students what else we have to offer. Though there could be some improvements in the realm of advocacy, fund-raising is where our club has made its most significant accomplishments.

Fund-Raising

Through a combination of university allotments and fund-raisers the club has been able to purchase a variety of items, most notably popular DVDs and best-selling novels of student choice for donation to the library. Few people enjoy fund-raisers, but if you need money to accomplish your club's goals they are certainly a viable option. And many fund-raisers do not require that you spend money up front to make money selling the product later. Instead, goods are received and paid for later, making these fund-raisers a good option for small groups with limited funds.

When we would hear the word "fund-raising," we would typically run, kicking and screaming, as far away as possible. But, for the club, we decided to do it anyway. The first few things you need to ask yourself when considering a fund-raiser are: What is best for your club, how much money would you like to raise, and how much time do you want to put into a fund-raiser? Once you answer these questions, you will be able to do a little bit of fund-raising research and then select the fund-raiser that is right for your club.

- KNOW THE RULES
  Before you start any fund-raiser make sure you know the rules. Find out what you can and cannot do according to the rules of your university. Have a good relationship with your student activities coordinator at your campus — this person can be an enormous help to you and your club when researching and coordinating your first fund-raiser. I, Marianne, have our activities coordinator on my IM so that when I am filling out paperwork or have a question I can send her an instant message and

get my answer right away. This is also a convenient way to bring club members in on the conversation if they're online too.

Make sure that you and one of your officers attend all the fund-raising meetings set up by your activities coordinator each semester so that you know all the fund-raising rules and any changes made from year to year. Always make sure to ask when you have a question, and remember that there are no stupid questions. We usually have four or five different meetings at our campus, so each of the four officers attends one meeting with me. These meetings bring together club officers and advisors and gives them an opportunity to work together, ultimately infusing new ideas into to each organization. Here, you can get fund-raising ideas from others, and also learn from their mistakes. These meetings also offer an opportunity to ask other advisors how they motivate their club members to do fund-raising.

- Putting the "Fun" in Fund-raising

Few people like to sell — and being good at it is a special talent. Personally, we both cringe at the thought of selling. Some would rather just donate money, but there are times when you must sell to raise the funds you need. When you start thinking about holding a fund-raiser, meet with your club members and throw some suggestions around. You will be astonished by how many good ideas your club members have. Candy, candles, cookie dough, pizza, subs, magazines ... on and on you go, one idea after another. Whatever idea you end up choosing, you must make sure that you have everyone's full agreement to sell. Often you find two or three members who really go out of their way to sell and the rest of the club members sell one or two items or none at all. But *everyone* has to make a commitment to sell.

One strategy that has always worked for us is to make it into a competition, awarding a prize to top sellers. For the prize I would simply pay a visit to the campus bookstore and stock up on university paraphernalia. I would buy Penn State mugs and fill them with Penn State magnets, candy, gum, pencils and pens, and sticky notes. Then the one club member who really excels and puts forth a tremendous effort is rewarded with a Penn State T-shirt. In addition, check to see if any prizes are awarded by the vendor providing the fund-raiser items. You might be surprised to read that students can be seduced into selling more just by offering a few small tokens, but give it a try. We hope you find that it works for you, too.

The first year the Library Student Advisory Board had a fund-raiser we sold candles. (Check with your student affairs office before selling these; some campuses may ban the sale of candles.) We made some money from this fund-raiser, but it was all on the backs of two or three students. A representative of the company gave a candle gift basket to the student who sold the most merchandise. The next year the students wanted to try something different (and candles and candle sales were banned from campus), so one came up with the idea of selling Penn State Schuylkill long-

Library Student Advisory Board's fund-raiser items: stadium blankets, scarves, and long-sleeve T-shirts.

sleeve T-shirts, scarves, and stadium blankets. This was a big hit on campus because the campus store did not sell any clothing items with the name "Schuylkill" on them; everything just said "Penn State." The company we bought from embroidered the Nittany Lion and "Penn State Schuylkill" on the items we selected. Because this company worked in our hometown and its owners were Penn State fans, they gave us a special deal. We sold out the first week and our treasurer had to order more. The second year we sold knit caps and scarves with "Penn State Schuylkill" and the Nittany Lion embroidered on them, which were also good sellers.

Our third year we decided to get away from the clothing line and sell Hershey candy bars. The company that we dealt with was wonderful and it was very easy to do. You could purchase different cases depending on what type of candy bars you wanted: Skittles, Twizzlers, M & Ms, Hershey Milk Chocolate Bars, etc. We had eight small boxes to a case and you could purchase any amount of cases at a time. You could even purchase one case at a time, if that is what you wanted. Each candy bar cost you $0.50 and then you sold them for $1 each, doubling your initial investment. As a bonus, inside each candy bar was a coupon for $1 off at Subway, making them an even easier sell. As you might expect, candy bars are very popular with students.

The candy did not last long, doubling our money in no time. Regardless of what you decide to use as your fund-raiser, make sure that you and your students are in agreement about what to sell and make sure you get *everyone* involved.

Keep in mind that fund-raising is supposed to be a moneymaker, so do make sure that you are charging enough. As James Swan says in *Fundraising for Libraries*, "A reasonable price is whatever a willing buyer and a willing seller agree upon."[1] For example, our club purchased navy-blue beanies with "Penn State Schuylkill" embroidered on the front. Each cap cost us $5, and the club sold them for $10, making a $5 profit on each cap. The club members wanted to make sure that they made a profit, but they also wanted to sell the items at a fair price so that college students could afford them. If you find items aren't moving, you can always lower the price later.

Another potential fund-raiser is a white elephant sale, or rummage table. Just be sure to check your rules and regulations about selling donated items before planning a sale. This is a great idea for a weekend, avoiding the typical weekday conflicts like classes, workshops, and club meetings. Ask the campus community members if they have any items that they would like to get rid of. Send out an e-mail or distribute flyers to everyone on campus to let them know what your club is planning and ask for their help. Most people jump at the chance to get rid of the junk in their basement, closet, or garage. In addition, remember the wise old saying: one person's trash is another's treasure. You could even hold this event at the end of your spring semester so that students packing up and leaving for the summer, especially those living on campus, can eliminate some of the things they have collected during the year and don't want to haul back home. You do not have to accept every donation, accept only the contributions that you think you can sell. This idea is great because it will cost you nothing but your time. Schedule your students accordingly so that you will not be the only one staffing your tables. Have your treasurer find a safe place to store your money during the sale, such as a lockbox or anything offering some security. Most local newspapers have classifieds that let you advertise neighborhood events for free. Take advantage of this and put a small blurb in the newspaper about your club's event. You could even go so far as to post flyers in nearby towns and put up signs along the roads leading to campus. Whatever you decide to call your sale — whether it is a garage, rummage, or white elephant sale — people *will* come. Price your items appropriately. Remember that you want to make money but keep in mind that you are selling someone else's discards.

Occasionally you may come across big-ticket items that you can ask a good price for, like a stereo or media cabinet. Some of your customers may want to try to negotiate the price with you. If you would be uncomfortable with this, have a "Fund-raising Event, All Prices Final" sign. If prices will be negotiable, have a discussion with your members before the sale and agree on how much you will be willing to go down in price—10 percent, 20 percent, 50 percent lower than marked? Find someone with a talent for negotiating to handle any tough sales or big-ticket items. There are also hundreds of Web sites out there that will offer tips on holding a successful yard sale. Have fun!

Raffle tickets and bingo are two more fund-raiser ideas. Before doing any kind of fund-raiser that involves gambling (including sale of raffle tickets, bingo, or casino night) check the rules and regulations not only with your student affairs department, but also with your township or state. Find out what the laws are for the specific type of fund-raiser you would like to do. You might need to get a special permit for these kinds of events.

When we wanted to do a raffle, we called our county courthouse and asked for the facts on gambling for fund-raisers. They sent us a packet of information with the rules and regulations for holding any kind of gambling event. In our case, the club needed to vote on whether to have a raffle and we needed to provide a copy of our meeting minutes with the outcome of the vote, along with a list of members and their phone numbers. Our application paperwork needed to be notarized before submission, but once we had the permit it was good for a year and others on campus could also use it. The only drawback in our case was that the person signing the permit, the Library Student Advisory Board advisor, has to be present at all functions making use of the permit, including those held by other campus clubs.

Sub sales are also an excellent way to build up your club's coffers, and if you sell vouchers you won't even have to worry about handling or delivering the product. With voucher-type sub sales you just sell tickets and collect the money and the purchasers pick up their own subs at the restaurant by a certain date. Check with your community sub and pizza shops. With any luck you will find that most eateries will work with you on a fund-raiser. You get to make some money and they get some free advertising and new customers.

It might seem a little unconventional, but Avon also has a great fund-raiser that you could use. We have a student in our club who sells Avon. Most likely you know someone too. All you do for Avon is show the catalog, take down the order, and collect the money. When the order comes in, it comes to you prepackaged in an Avon bag with the purchaser's name right on it and you only have to hand them out. Avon gives 40 percent of the sales to your club. Today Avon has something for everyone; they even carry men's products now. Our area schools have used Avon for fund-raisers and have done very well.

There are also ways to hold a fund-raiser without selling a thing. In our first year the club decided to have a car wash. We were granted permission to use the parking lot, and the maintenance department provided buckets and arranged for us to connect hoses to a nearby water spout. An area business donated the sponges and soap, so the only investment on behalf of the club was time — the donations were all

We had plenty of help at our fourth annual car wash, 2007.

profit. We held the car wash from noon to 4:00 P.M. and students scheduled themselves to help out between classes. We got everyone involved and had a great time. The day was beautiful and we did extremely well. We did so well that at our next meeting we voted to make the car wash an annual event. The next year we expanded our car wash idea to include a valet service. Many faculty and staff could not leave their offices during the scheduled time, so the library staff volunteered to set up times to pick up their cars, wash them, and return them. This was a hit. We found that we made more money by simply asking for a donation than asking for a fixed dollar amount. Donations were boosted with the valet service because many also gave tips. However, before offering the valet service, check with your campus or your personal insurance provider about insurance coverage in the event of an accident while driving someone else's car. If you're not covered, it is probably not a liability you want personally to be responsible for.

We picked the month of September for our car wash because it is still warm and rain is at a minimum. Also, the students are still enthusiastic because school has just started and they are not yet into mid-terms or finals. If you have new members in the club, this is also great way for them to make friends. Working together to get people to come to the car wash and get the cars clean has been a real bonding experience for our members. We have some competition with other clubs holding car washes in September, but in our region spring weather can be unpredictable and in

April or May students are more concerned about finals and summer vacation plans than raising money for the club.

You could also go "canning" for your club, soliciting cash donations at places like Wal-Mart, shopping malls, or even door-to-door. We did this to raise money for the dance marathon ("THON"), where canning is a tradition and a rite of passage for participants. Before you go, check the campus rules and regulations and take student safety into consideration. Also be sure to arrange the details in advance with the store or mall manager. Some stores may contribute or even double the amount you collect, so do ask the manager about this when you call.

If your students go canning, make sure that they wear bright clothing (preferably with the university logo), carry their student IDs, and that all cans display information about the club and the fund-raiser, including the phone number and Web site URL if you have one. All students must follow the vehicle code of your city and state. In our state this means we must never stand in the middle of the street, walk on the medians, or solicit after dark. The safety of students is the most important

Penn State University's annual dance marathon (THON), which is held in State College, Pennsylvania. THON was started in 1973 and has raised more than $46 million for the Four Diamonds Fund, benefiting child cancer patients at the Penn State Hershey Children's Hospital in Hershey, Pennsylvania.

Loni Picarella, president of LSAB 2006, dancing at THON.

thing. With this in mind, it is also a good idea for club members to go canning in pairs or small groups. Some campuses might require your students to sign waivers, so check to see what the requirements are at your school.

We recruited the university mascot to join us at our event and hand out balloons. This was a big hit with the children and their parents, and a great photo opportunity for some. Remind students that they are representing their campus and university and should act accordingly. Also remind them that they may be recruiting new students in the process.

Grants

As some readers may already know, a lot of work goes into preparing a grant and it does take some skill. The work involved doesn't exactly make grant money "free," but at least it is money that doesn't have to be paid back. And while you stand to receive more money from grants than fund-raising, there are no guarantees in grants. You may decide that your time is better spent on a small-scale fund-raiser with guarantee of some return on the time invested. Or, maybe you will decide to take the gamble. Grant proposals are not something our club has seriously considered yet, but your club may want to pursue a grant for a special collection or hosting a special event.

Some of the questions you might have before vying for a grant are:

- Where do I start researching grants?
- Is our club eligible for grants?
- How much money will I be able to receive? How much do we want to request?
- Do we have the time to invest in this?

To find answers to these questions we suggest you start by speaking with staff in the research or development office on your campus. They may offer workshops on grant writing or even be able to help you write your grant. If not, watch for grant writing programs offered by your state or local library association. In addition, you may wish to explore opportunities to attend the Grants 101 workshop offered by the Grant Institute (www.thegrantinstitute.com). See the recommended reading list at the end of this chapter for more information.

Charting Your Course: Planning for the Future

Once all certificates of appreciation have been awarded, you have had your big group hug, and said goodbye to those members leaving you, you need to take a deep breath and start planning for next year. But in reality, planning for next year starts even before students leave for the summer. Each year you will need to hold elections at the time designated in your club's constitution. Typically, this will be at the end of the school year. Once you hold elections, get your new officers together and develop a great plan of action for next year. Try to include your officers in summer activities, if possible, to help keep them excited and motivated for the next year. When students return in the fall, have a meeting with your new officers to finalize plans for upcoming events, such as the club's first meeting, campus activities fair, or club car wash. Make sure that they know they are welcome to come and talk to you at any time.

There have been some semesters when we only needed to replace one or two officers and others when we have had to replace all four. Starting with a fresh slate of officers can be a very difficult time; it can feel like you are starting your club all over again. For each new leader you will have to do training and thoroughly discuss with each exactly what their position entails and what your expectations are. But new leaders also bring their own unique personalities and can bring a lot of great new ideas to the group. Some students really shine when they step up into a leadership position and others might need some guidance and encouragement. Be sure to keep in touch with them regularly during this transition time. You may find that in no time at all your new leaders will take over their job duties with ease and confidence.

The Library Student Advisory Board

Advisor's Job Over the Summer

Okay, it's the end of the year, the kids are gone, you have the whole summer ahead of you. Take a deep breath, exhale ... take another deep breath, and exhale again. Now back to work! You may wish to complete some of the actions described below before the students leave. Have the students provide as much help as possible with these.

- Take out the minutes from each monthly meeting reread them. We bet you will be amazed at how much your club accomplished. We always overlook some of the activities we did during the year. Reviewing the evidence in the minutes helps remind us. Compile for your records a list of everything your club did: fund-raiser totals, special events, field trips, allocations the club received, displays that were created, support provided to other clubs, donations, etc. Then, send this report of all the club's activities to your library administrators and your student affairs department. It sounds like a lot of work, but this is actually one of our favorite times of the year. It's fun to review our achievements.

- If possible, select dates for next year's meetings and special events. Then meet with your student affairs director and go over this schedule to get club events on the campus calendar. If your event conflicts with another, you may wish to change the date. You will find, however, that some conflict will be unavoidable.

- Once you have dates selected for meetings and special events, complete your room and equipment request forms. Be sure to keep copies of these on file and have them readily available on the day of the event in case of problems.

- Go over your treasurer's reports. Make sure that any funds that won't carry over to next year are spent. Verify all balances with the student affairs department. File away old receipts with a copy of the past year's transactions.

- Get a head start on fund-raising by looking into potential fund-raisers and compile a list for your first meeting. You may even be able to get a jump start on fund-raising by selecting a fall fund-raiser at your very first meeting of the year.

- As the fall semester draws near, start to prepare for recruiting and the return of club members. Make some eye-catching posters, flyers, and bookmarks to attract students to your table at the first activities fair, or similar event on your campus. Bookmarks with our library club's name, advisor's e-mail address, and library hours are popular with our students. See some samples in Appendix B.

The summer months are typically slow and are a good time work on any plans for the upcoming year. This is the perfect time to get those little extras done while your students are away. Try to involve interested members of the library staff during the summer when workloads may be a little lighter. They may also enjoy making posters, as well as planning fund-raisers and special events. We often see grant opportunities, award nominations, and contests advertised during the summer. Your club might consider applying for grants or entering contests with prizes that could be donated to the library. If one of your new, or even past, student leaders happens to be around during the summer, taking a lead role on projects like these can be a great way for them to develop their leadership skills. If you don't have any club members on campus over the summer months, consider taking advantage of these opportunities yourself, on behalf of the club. Rather than relying solely on internal funding and fund-raisers, ask your club to invest a little time in grant seeking to increase their buying power.

As mentioned at the beginning of this chapter, it is important to stay in contact with your members over the summer. Most of your club members will probably be away from campus over the summer — returning home to work, spend time with family and old friends, do an internship, or perhaps travel. Sending a message every few weeks, or whenever you have an update to share, keeps them interested in the club and reminds them that someone back at campus is thinking of them. This can also be a good time to get to know more about your students. In your messages, ask them what they have been up to. Though you may only get a few responses, through these messages you can find out new skills or adventures the club might be able to capitalize on later.

The beginning of the fall semester is one of the busiest times for an advisor — it is often one of the busiest times of the year for *everyone* on campus. Students are anxiously waiting to start the new school year — taking new classes, making new friends, and joining new clubs. This is the time when you really want to be most prepared. Toward the end of the summer, before the students start arriving, send an e-mail to your returning club members. Tell them to come by and visit when they get to campus, ask them how their summer went, and let them know how glad you are they are coming back to start the beginning of a prosperous new year for the library club. Get them excited about their library student advisory board.

As the summer draws to a close, start preparing for the first meetings of the fall. Make sure any paperwork needing to be submitted at the beginning of the semester is finished and ready to go. Before the deposits and withdrawals to the club's funds start happening in the fall, check with the person in charge of your club's ledger balances to make sure the library club's account balances are accurate. We do this a few times a year. It is also good to have an accurate starting balance at the beginning of the semester for your treasurer. In our case, supply money is usually automatically deposited at the beginning of the semester, so it is important to make sure that these funds were received and recorded by the treasurer.

The end of the summer is also when we usually take all of the paperwork for the previous year — information on donations, receipts, events, fund-raisers, meeting sign-in sheets and minutes — and file it away in a large, dated folder or envelope. A new folder is then created for the upcoming year.

Start out fresh with the names of your returning members and officers. Double check your calendars for all the meeting and event dates that you signed up for. Remind your students of all the important upcoming dates, meeting times, and events that you voted on the previous semester. Have any fund-raiser ideas and materials requested over the summer ready to hand out and discuss with your club. Make sure all members, new and old, have a copy of your club's constitution. Get handouts ready for any member-recruitment opportunities, such as our activities fair usually held the first week school is in session. Have those posters out that you have been working on over the summer. Finally, review any room arrangement or equipment requests for meetings and special events made in the spring or over the summer with the corresponding department to avoid any surprises on the day of the event.

Recommended Reading

Barber, Peggy, and Linda D. Crowe. *Getting Your Grant: A How-To-Do-It Manual for Librarians.* New York: Neal-Schuman, 1993.

Written with libraries in mind, readers will find good advice and examples most can relate to. Included is practical advice for identifying funding sources and strategies for seeking funding from government, foundation, and corporate sources. Also included are the basic components of a grant, hints for securing your grants, and samples to use as a guide.

Bell, Arthur H., and Dayle M. Smith. *Motivating Yourself for Achievement.* Upper Saddle River, NJ: Prentice Hall, 2003.

Everything you want to know about self-motivation is here. This book helps you understand the meaning of motivation and provides exercises to help improve your skills. It's a quick read and very informative.

Gerding, Stephanie K., and Pamela H. MacKellar. *Grants for Libraries: A How-To-Do-It Manual for Librarians.* New York: Neal-Schuman, 2006.

This book brings together many best practices and models for grant writing in libraries. In some ways it updates and expands upon Barber & Crowe's *Getting Your Grant,* though readers may find it beneficial to also review this earlier title. The Gerding and MacKellar book is broken into three large sections: a review of the grant process, including completed examples; real-life success stories; and how to create your own grant using the tools provided.

Herring, Mark Youngblood. *Raising Funds with Friends Groups.* **New York: Neal-Schuman, 2004.**

This book relates to friends groups in the traditional sense. It offers great ideas and suggestions for ways to raise funds and market your library.

Karsh, Ellen, and Arlen Sue Fox. *The Only Grant-Writing Book You'll Ever Need.* **New York: Carroll & Graf, 2006.**

An easy-to-read book that takes you through preparation, proposal writing, and follow-up, this books chapters are actually individual lessons, so if you can't attend a grant-writing workshop this could be a great substitute. Though this book contains fewer examples of completed proposals than other books, it does contain a lot of practical information for the novice grant writer.

Ward, Deborah, ed. *Writing Grant Proposals That Win.* **Sudbury, MA: Jones and Barlett, 2006.**

This book does not focus on grant writing from a library perspective. However, it does offer tips on reading the grant's request for proposal and writing your grant, as well as what reviewers are looking for and how they function. After looking at the *How-To for Librarians* books, serious grant writers will want to examine this book too.

7

Promote and Recruit

Get the Word Out on Campus

It is important to get the word out on campus about your library student advisory board so that students — as well as faculty and staff— become aware of the club, its activities, and how it can improve the student campus experience. There are many ways of spreading the word, including special displays, posters, activities fairs, showing off club members' talents at special events, and more. Spreading the word on campus is a great way to make use of some of those special talents you have discovered among your members. You will be surprised by how many students want to show their artistic and computer skills by volunteering for these projects. For additional ideas on marketing your library and your club, see "Recommended Reading" at the end of this chapter. Examples of some of the techniques we have used follow.

One way you can advertise your club is to secure usage rights to a display case on campus, somewhere centrally located but not in the library. Find the department in charge of the display case and ask if your club might use it to create a display of your club's activities, along with a call to join. In our case there is a showcase in our student center, between the cafeteria and auditorium. This is one of the busiest places on campus. Make a colorful exhibit about your club, what it has accomplished, what it wants to accomplish, and what the club can do for students. Use big, bold, colorful lettering to catch the eyes of the students, staff, and faculty — but avoid having too much text. We even displayed the products from our fund-raisers to make the entire campus community aware of what we are selling. Be sure to include e-mail addresses and phone numbers so students can get in touch with you or your club officers.

Have club members make colorful posters, flyers, and pamphlets and hang them on bulletin boards in the student center, classroom hallways, student housing — any place on campus where they can be seen. (Some institutions stipulate that you must have all public signage approved.) Our club is allotted supply money each year just for this purpose.

Above: Spring 2007 LSAB members, from left: Hannah Tracy, Tyray Solomon, Taren West, Elizabeth Yocom, Felicia O'Connor, R.J. Wawrzyniakowski, Josh Perreault, Alieshia King, Leah Kraft and Brittany Mitchell. *Below*: Maureen Ketner (left), president, and Leah Kraft, vice president, showing examples of the READ poster created for our annual National Library Week display.

Using READ Posters

Another way to advertise your club is by making READ posters using image files available for purchase from the American Library Association. This CD-ROM gives you instructions for making both posters and bookmarks and allows you some creative flexibility. Using these files require use and knowledge of image-editing software. You may find that you have image-editing software on your computer that you just weren't aware of or haven't used. Contact your IT department to see what is available to you, or purchase popular software such as Adobe Photoshop. There are many students who are already familiar with this program. However, if you are not familiar with image-editing software it may be in your best interest to learn it yourself. Your campus IT department may even offer beginning and advanced training classes you can take. If you at least learn the basics for using the program, you will have the security of knowing that you do not have to rely solely on your students to create and revise your club's posters — often a different student each year. There is much to learn, but it is well worth your trouble.

- ### PREPARATION TIPS FOR CREATING READ POSTERS

Any type of photo-editing software can seem a little intimidating at first. If you do not have online or in-house training classes offered by your university, you can simply use your software's "Help" tools to learn how to manipulate photographs to incorporate them with the images provided on the American Library Association (ALA) READ CDs. I, Marianne, was able to take a self-paced online course in Adobe Photoshop through my university where I learned a lot about how to use the image-editing program, but I still found the Adobe Help Center useful for the tasks needed

Jordan Seiler, LSAB president, 2003 (creator of the READ posters) and Marianne Seiler, LSAB advisor, standing with posters featuring faculty and administration.

Jonathan Seiler, U.S. Navy Reservist and history major.

Maureen Ketner, chemical engineering and chemistry major.

Felishia O'Connor, nursing major.

Ashley Fehr, English major.

READ poster featuring Penn State Schuylkill faculty and their publications. From left: Dr. Camilla Kari, assistant professor of humanities and speech communications; Dr. Anita Vickers, associate professor of humanities and English; and Dr. Judy Stephens, professor of humanities and theater.

READ poster featuring Penn State Schuylkill's Chef/Supervisor, Chef Penny Shade.

to create a nice poster. I have found that these tutorials can be very helpful not just for first-time users, but also for quick reference help.

The Adobe Help Center has a list of tutorials that you can use to get started with creating your READ posters. They give you information on colors and tones, how to correct defects in your pictures, using layers, and adding shapes. They also offer more advanced tutorials when you are ready for them. Start out easy at first and work your way to more advanced creations. Have fun with this program, experiment, and enjoy.

One of our Library Student Advisory Board members, Anthony Phillips, does a fantastic job creating our posters with Adobe Photoshop and has written a how-to guide to help you get started. But first, some tips on taking those photographs of the people you want to feature in your READ posters.

- TAKING THE PICTURE
    - If you want to make a large poster (similar to the celebrity READ posters for sale at the ALA Store), we recommend maximizing your results by using your digital camera's highest resolution setting — whatever it may be. These files will take up a lot of memory on your camera card and your computer's hard drive when you transfer the file, but it's a lot easier to reduce the file size later (using your photo editing software) than to improve the image's quality later on.
    - Make sure your subject's head and shoulders are completely within the shot. A photo with the top of the head or sides of the shoulders cut off are awkward to place in the poster. We have found that a shot of our subject from the waist up, either sitting or standing, is ideal. If you have a lower-resolution camera, the closer you can get to your subject, the more likely you will be to get sharp facial features when you blow up the image.
    - Place your subject in front of a solid background with high contrast to their clothing and skin tone. This will make your job of editing the photo later much easier.
    - Make sure your subject is well lit, avoiding shadows as much as possible.

Creating a READ Poster
by Anthony Phillips

- Now that you have your picture it is time to get to the real work. First, upload the photographs you have just taken, onto your computer. Save the pictures on your computer in a place where you can easily find them, in a folder with a meaningful name. Once the pictures have been saved on your computer, you may wish to rename the files to include the name of your subject so they are easy to find again later.

- Now open the picture within Adobe Photoshop or the photo-editing software of your choice. You have two ways of doing this.

  - Right click on the picture (double click for Macs), drag your cursor down to the option entitled "open with," and choose the program you wish to use. If you don't see your program on the list, then drag your cursor to the option "choose program" and choose Adobe Photoshop or whichever program you choose to use from the list.

  - Or, open Adobe Photoshop, or whichever program you will be using. Once the program is open, drag your cursor to the menu bar and choose "File," scroll down to the option "Open," and choose the picture from its saved location.

- Picture open, now it's time to get to editing and creating a masterpiece, right? Whoa! Hold your horses, now, before you get to that editing. Let's make sure that your work space is ready. First take your cursor, drag it to the menu bar, and bring it to the option entitled "Window" and click on it. Here is what you are looking for: you want the options entitled "Tool," "Layers," and "History" to have a check next to them. This will put the editing tools you will need on your screen. (Note: the remaining instructions are for using Adobe Photoshop. Please use your program's "Help" files to learn how to do the remaining steps using your software.)

- Let's make sure that you still have everything that you will need to get the job done:

  - Picture open
  - Tool bar displayed
  - Layer window displayed
  - History window displayed

- Now for what you have been waiting for — the actual creation of the poster. Let's go through this step by step. First let's edit the background out of the photo, leaving us with the person we want to insert in front of one of the READ backgrounds.

  - Make sure your picture is the active window by clicking on it to select it. Then, on your keyboard press F7 to create a new layer so that you can do more work.

  - Drag your cursor to the "Tool" window and click on one of these two options:

    - If you took your photograph with a solid background that is in contrast to the clothes and skin color of your subject, you can do this the easy way. Drag the cursor the option entitled the "Magic Wand" (it is the one that looks like a stick with sparks coming from it). Yes, that's it. Now take your cursor, which should have turned into the magic wand, and place it anywhere on the background portion of your photograph and left click. There should now be dotted lines going around the subject, encasing the background. Now press the "Delete" or "Backspace" key on your keyboard. Calm down, you didn't mess up the picture! The black space behind the picture is a good thing, because now you can insert your READ background.

- If you are a more technical person, there is another way. Drag your cursor to the "Tool" window and place it over the option entitled "Lasso Tool." Left click on it, but don't release the mouse button. Hold the button down, and from there drag your cursor down to the option entitled "Magnetic Lasso." This tool allows you do the same as the magic wand, except with this tool you have to manually highlight the border of the background. This way you can catch details of the person or the book that might be cut out using the Magic Wand. It might help to zoom in a little bit on your photograph when using this method. After you finish highlighting the border press "Delete" and you should be left with the blank background just like with the magic wand.

- Time for the final steps.

  - Drag your cursor to the menu bar and click on the "File" option. Choose the "Open" option and browse to select the image of the background that you want to use for your poster. If your READ files came on a CD, make sure the CD is in your computer's CD-ROM drive. Now with this image drag your cursor to the "Layers" window and right next to the one image layer that is down there you will see a lock symbol. The lock symbol means that the image is locked, and for these you must click on the lock in order to unlock it for editing.

  - Drag your cursor onto your READ background image, then click and drag the image into the original picture (the person) that you were working with. Now if you can't see the picture that you were originally working with, you have to drag your cursor onto the layers window and rearrange the layers so that image that the one you were working with is in front of the background. Doing this is just a simple process of dragging and dropping the layers in the "Layers" window.

  - Finally, drag your cursor over to the "Tool" window and click on the big letter "T" to activate the text. From there you can type the words "Read" or any additional text you might want on the poster, such as the person's name. Have fun and play around with text until you get the words just how you like it.

- There you go — your very own READ poster. Make sure to save your work!

In our very first year the club created and displayed READ posters featuring faculty, holding either their published works or their favorite books, to help raise library awareness during National Library Week. The students had fun making the posters and the faculty enjoyed being a part of the activities. This interaction of students and faculty helped the campus population become aware of what the club can do for the library and campus community. During the club's third year we decided to do the READ posters again, this time using pictures of students and staff with their favorite books. Having staff pictured on the READ posters gives them the recognition they deserve for the wonderful jobs they do on campus and also lets the students become more acquainted with the campus staff. You may also find that just about all students recognize key members of the staff providing support services to students, while they may only recognize some of the faculty or fellow students.

Another way to promote the library club is by creating bookmarks with the club's name and advisor's contact information, along with the library's hours. Our club makes its bookmarks using Microsoft Word or Microsoft Publisher, both simple and easy to use for this purpose.[2] Have club members use their creativity when designing these bookmarks. We usually set the template to four bookmarks per 8.5" × 11" page. We then print them on the color printer purchased by the club for such purposes and laminate them to make them a little more durable. Once they are laminated, we have club members or student workers cut them to size. If your library or campus does not have a laminator, you could print them on colorful cardstock instead. We often do this to save time; the cardstock is a much heavier paper and holds up well. Another option would be to investigate having customized bookmarks professionally printed in bulk. Find an example of our bookmarks in Appendix B.

Since this is a *library* advisory board, you should have some club members with an interest in recreational reading. If you have club members who enjoy reading the latest best sellers, have them write a book review for the club newsletter, library newsletter, campus newsletter, or maybe even the local newspaper. Our library has a newsletter that we publish once each semester. It typically features updates on the newest technology in our library, highlights from the new books list, and a spotlight on a student worker. We have also started asking club members to write a review of a current best seller. Most best-selling novels are purchased by the club and donated to the library, so this also highlights the club's contribution to the library and raises awareness about the diversity of the club. Complementing their feature is a column reporting on the activities of the Library Student Advisory Board that semester. Other options would be to include reviews of the newest games or DVDs — any items purchased by the club for the library.

For those students who love cooking, ask them to do a feature on "recipes for the college student," or even a review of a special recipe Web site, cookbook, or interactive cooking DVD. The recipes should consider that students are often beginner chefs cooking in tight spaces with limited cooking paraphernalia, often have tight schedules, and that some students are seeking healthy, time-saving, or money-saving recipes. If dining options and cafeteria hours are limited, like at our campus, students will end up cooking at home some of the time. Some might even cook big meals for their friends on the weekends.

When our newsletter is finished, copies are published and placed in the student center, library, cafeteria, and dorms. We also make it available on the library's Web site and send out a link, along with highlights from the current issue, to the campus community.

In addition to the library newsletter, the club also publishes its own brag sheet. Remember, it is your newsletter — have fun with it! Talk with your students and see what they would like to read in a newsletter, or what they want other students to know about the club. If you have the resources, make your newsletter colorful. Keep the articles brief and upbeat. Once you do your first layout it is easy to fill in articles and pictures for your next publication. Our club uses Microsoft Publisher for our newsletters. It's easy to use and the templates give you many different design and color options. The result is a professional-looking newsletter that doesn't take a lot of time to create.

Supplementing the library and club newsletters, the LSAB maintains club-related pages on the library's Web site to share news and information about the club. Our pages display our club's monthly meeting dates for the semester, as well as dates and times of special events that will be taking place. We also include up-to-date pictures of club members and reports on activities, as well as officers' names, titles, and e-mail addresses. If anyone is interested in the club they can follow a link from any one of the officers' or the advisor's name to send an e-mail to get in contact with us.

We are working on expanding the Web site soon and intend to find a club member with web authoring skills to work on this project for the club. This is a good way to get your news out worldwide. Our Web site has a counter on it, which is helpful for gauging the site's use. If the count is low, consider better marketing, with links from other pages on your campus library Web site. Since our club has had its Web site, we have had numerous calls and e-mails from other academic libraries asking about what we do. After explaining to them our concept of a library club, we send examples of our constitution, bookmarks, flyers, and other publications. There is nothing quite like the feeling of having a phone call or an e-mail from another campus, or even a university in another state, to ask you about your club, how you got started, and how they can start their own library club. We have received numerous e-mails and phone calls from other Penn State campuses and academic libraries across the United States asking how to start a library club and for advice on keeping the students interested.

Simple word-of-mouth is another great way to spread the word on campus about your library club. Talk about your club to friends, coworkers, and campus administration. Keep faculty and staff aware of your organization's activities because they can become some of your best supporters. Other club advisors and members of the faculty come to us because we are known as the club that "gets it done." Have poetry readings, art shows, music fests, or poster contests in your library. The faculty will relish the idea of showing off their students' talents.

Another way to get the club in the faculty's good graces, if your library doesn't already do this, is to find out when a faculty member has had a book published, an album released, or an art exhibition and invite them to the library for a book or album signing, or to display their art work. Work with the campus bookstore to have copies for sale at the event. Have club members set up a table for refreshments. You want to have a good student turnout, so ask your students to spread the word among the student population on campus and bring their friends to the event. We were honored to have a published author as one of our club members. Elizabeth Yocom, a frosh, published a short novel as a high school senior and is working on her next book. We selected a day in March, coincidentally Women's History Month, and invited everyone to her book signing. This was a great opportunity to have students and faculty come together, honoring a student for her work. The club members really rallied with their support of a fellow student member and we had a great turnout.

Make sure to obtain or construct a calendar with your club's events that also includes everything else that is happening on campus. Use this to starting thinking about ways to get your club members involved with other organizations on campus. Encourage your club members to spread the word at their other meetings about the Library Student Advisory Board's special events. You will not have a good turnout at these events if students are not aware of the activity. Raising student awareness of campus events happens to be a bit of a problem on our campus. Too often we ask

Rosanne Chesakis, library assistant, introducing Elizabeth Yocom, LSAB member and author of *The Ritual and the Mages: The Battle Begins* at her book signing.

students why they weren't at a concert, movie, coffee house, or game night, and we hear in response, "I didn't know about that, that sounds awesome, I wish I [had known]." Special events, in particular, are where you need to employ all your advertising tactics — word of mouth, flyers, e-mails, posters, and Facebook (or other online social networking tools).

In past generations, and it may still continue today, colleges and universities often published "face books" containing photographs and names of students, faculty, and staff, intended to help them get to know each other. The online social network found at Facebook.com accomplishes the same thing, but in a contagious and continually evolving sort of way. It allows all members of a university community ("network") to create their online image ("profile") to share with other members of their network. More than just a face to put to a name, or a name to put to a face, it allows users to share likes and dislikes, current activities (such as membership in the campus Library Student Advisory Board), and more. Some students spend a great deal of time fine-tuning their profiles and managing their school and social lives, so it can be a great alternative to e-mail for alerting students about club activities. You can create a "group" for members of your club and remind them about club activities this way. Or, consider possible methods (and ethics of responsible use) for alerting all students in your network.

No, we are not Facebook junkies, although we do tend to update our photos

Elizabeth Yocom's book signing.

when we come across a thinner and younger depiction of ourselves. But honestly, Facebook is a good way to keep in contact with your students, meet new students, and post your club events. At the beginning of each semester we ask all new club members to join the Library Student Advisory Board's group on Facebook. This way we can keep in touch about upcoming events by posting them on the group's calendar of events. Facebook will also remind you about your contacts' birthdays, making it a great way to keep up with club members' birthdays. Be sure to wish your students a happy birthday and encourage others to do this. This adds a personal touch and makes the student feel cared for. We can also keep in touch with students from other universities who have similar interests in library issues and events. Until something bigger and better comes along, which is inevitable, you will likely find most or even all of your club members are already using Facebook before they even arrive on campus.

During the Summer Months

During the summer months we often have students taking summer courses at our campus who are also at home working over the summer. A number of these students, who attend other campuses throughout the rest of the year, have remarked on the "personality" of our library. The other day one student commented, "Do you realize how wonderful your library is? I love to study here; your library is relaxing and idyllic. We can snack and talk in our study groups and are not told to be quiet! I wish our library could be like this — I would be there all the time." So we explained about our Library Student Advisory Board and that our club members have a voice in the library. We told her about the changes that the library has made in just four short years and that the student members raise money to purchase items for students that an academic library might not allocate the funding for, such as DVDs, best sellers, color printers, etc. The student took notes and plans to go before her library administration to see if the students at her campus could also have a voice in the library and change the all-too-familiar attitude of library administrators still living in the past. Our library gave her a sample packet containing different handouts and flyers that explain what our club does, a copy of our recent club newsletter, and a sample bookmark we make to promote the club. We also talked to her about going to her campus student affairs department to find out the rules and regulations for starting a club at her school.

Recruit New Members Throughout the Year

The promotional ideas presented at the beginning of this chapter should not only help you spread awareness about your club, but also help you recruit new members.

And it is important to try to recruit new members throughout the year. Students' interests and schedules can quickly change. When they hear from friends about what the club is doing, attend a special event hosted by the club, or borrow popular materials from the library that were donated by the club, they very well may become interested in joining themselves. Or in the spring semester their schedules may change so that they can now attend club meetings that they couldn't attend in the fall. Make sure students know you are *always* interested in receiving new members to the club.

Kick off the year by planning to host a table at your campus student activities fair. This is a great way to easily recruit new students to your club. Our campus holds an activities fair, an opportunity for students to shop for student clubs, at the beginning of each semester to encourage students to get involved on campus. Your campus is likely to have a similar event.

Have club members interact with fellow students at the event to get them interested in your club. Make colorful displays to attract the students to your table — have balloons; eye-catching, colorful posters; and little handouts like wristbands, key chains, tablets, pencils, and candy. We also made a display of our READ posters and had a drawing to pick lucky students to be featured on their own 23" × 35" poster. Somewhat surprisingly, we found that many students were eager to be featured in a poster to be hung in the library and elsewhere around campus. Also, consider distributing bookmarks with your library hours, Web site URL, e-mail address, and phone number. Even if they are not interested in joining the club, it is great to be able to get this information out to as many students as possible. Finally, if you are currently doing fund-raisers, display and sell your merchandise. Have a sign-up sheet for names and e-mail addresses so that you can immediately update your membership list. Following the event, send out an e-mail announcing your new members and welcome them to the club. Let them know when your next meeting is and — *keep in touch!*

Sending presidents of other clubs invitations to your club meetings is another way to recruit new members and build new relationships. Invite them to one of your monthly meetings and tell them that you would like them to meet your club. This can open up a whole new world of opportunities. You will find that the other club presidents are honored to be invited to your meetings. As a result of this we have had at least three presidents from other clubs ask to join our Library Student Advisory Board.

One way to recruit, spread the word, and keep members motivated all at the same time is to get your club members involved with other clubs and activities. From students' early years at high school through their years in college they will often hear, "Get involved! Get the full college experience!" Many members of our club are already involved with social or educational clubs on campus. Some are even involved with the Student Government Association (SGA), which decides how additional funds are allotted to student clubs. Students will inevitably talk about the library club at other club meetings, spreading the word about the club and potentially recruiting new members and building new partnerships. This involvement helps the students to work together for the good of the whole campus. Remember, even though you are a library club you are all working to improve your campus as a whole.

For example, one of our vice presidents represented both our club and our campus at the Penn State Dance Marathon, or "THON" as it is called (http://thon.org). THON is reportedly the largest student-run philanthropy in the world. The dance marathon was started in 1973; proceeds of the event were first donated to the Four Diamonds Fund in 1977 and in 1978 a permanent relationship with the Four Diamonds Fund was established. Since then, students have raised more than $51 million for the fund. This fund benefits child cancer patients at the Penn State Hershey Children's Hospital in Hershey, Pennsylvania, by providing care and family support, as well as funding research. Not only was our club linked with this incredible fundraising event, but it also provided an opportunity for the club to raise awareness of our group's activities to peers across the university system. Also, the two students representing our campus were able to feel a strong sense of belonging to the Penn State

Policy meeting of the Student Affairs Department.

community. The event's 700 dancers, plus hundreds of student-event staff and supporters easily outnumber our campus's total student population. This was an experience like no other!

Because of our reputation on campus as the club that gets things done, faculty seek us out to help provide assistance in getting students involved in art shows, jazz fests, and author book signings. We were recently asked by the campus Faculty Organization's Information Systems Committee[3] if one of our club members would represent the student population by joining the committee. This is a great opportunity for students to have a voice in faculty initiatives. Our club was also selected to participate in Penn State Schuylkill's Open House Panel Discussion and Activities Display for prospective students. These diverse activities help bring new and exciting pursuits to members and keep your club from becoming stale. In addition, our club has sponsored a bus trip to a jazz fest for our campus music professor and his students, and we were called upon by a professor of kinesiology to help with the annual Gladiator Games. Even though these are not all library-related events, we are able to introduce ourselves and get the word out about our library club. As a result we have successfully signed up new recruits. This increases awareness of our club and encourages both the commuter students and the on-campus students to interact more with each other — an important concern at our campus.

Recommended Reading

Woodward, Jeannette. *Creating the Customer-Driven Library: Building on the Bookstore Model.* Chicago: American Library Association, 2005.

If you're looking for a book on displays, lighting, signage, customer service, publicity for your library, Web site design, and much more — this is the book to read. It gives wonderful ideas on how to market your library.

8

Club Activities

When we were getting the club started, one of the first questions we asked ourselves was how the club could help us make our library more welcoming to our students. Attractive potted plants or flower arrangements to make it homier? Comfy chairs and sofas? Different lighting? What would the students suggest? Throughout the book we have mentioned some examples. In this chapter we will focus on how the club's activities benefit the library, campus, and community. Since its inception, the work of our Library Student Advisory Board has expanded. Though this may not be the outcome we expected in the beginning, we feel that the students' library advocacy ultimately has a more powerful effect on our relationship with the student body than simply offering ideas to the library administration. Evidence shows that they have encouraged more students to come to the library, perhaps without even realizing. Once they are in the library it is our responsibility to show students what we have to offer, to get them to stay at the library, and convince them to return often.

Activities Contributing to the Library

In the beginning, all of the club's activities focused on the library. It wasn't until later — when we encouraged the direction of the club to expand with the interests of the members and when others on campus began to take notice of the success of our Library Student Advisory Board — that the club began to focus on activities outside the library.

Café Campaign

Our first group of club members asked for coffee, soda, and snack machines in the library. At the time we had already converted a small area of the library into a café, but the coffee cart provided by campus food services never received quite enough business to warrant the staffing and the cart was removed. The area was already decorated with watercolors and charcoal drawings on loan to the library, bistro tables accented with bud vases, and a decorative rug. New issues of daily newspapers and

The "Hardback Café," located on the first floor of the Ciletti Memorial Library, Penn State Schuylkill.

popular magazines lured patrons into the area. It just lacked some snacks to munch on while people relaxed. We were able to act on this simple suggestion to get some caffeine and snacks back in the library by going through the proper channels, and to do it at no cost to the library club. This has since become a hot spot in our library.

To some this might seem insignificant, but it was a big deal in our little library. It was a little change that helped make the library seem more comfortable and attracted a few more people into the building. When you're on a budget, word of forty-five-cent coffee and hot chocolate spreads quickly. And honestly, it tasted pretty good.

If you don't already have a café in your library, a naming contest can help attract attention for your grand opening. We had a contest to name our new café. This was very exciting for students, staff, and faculty. We placed a decorated voting box at the library circulation desk for a month and we sent out flyers and e-mails telling everyone about the contest to give them a chance to vote for their favorite name. Our selection committee consisted of students, faculty, and staff on campus. The committee discussed the names and picked "Hardback Café" as the name. The winner of the contest was awarded a gift certificate to an area restaurant.

Games and Puzzles

First-year club members also suggested that the library have some games or puzzles for students. So we now have puzzles — typically 500 to 1,000 pieces — in a bright, open area of the library for anyone to pass the time between classes or take a study break to clear their minds. We typically put out one puzzle at a time, putting out a new puzzle when the previous one is completed. This is an inexpensive and fun way to enhance your library's atmosphere. You will be amazed at how many people have puzzles just sitting around their homes and will donate them to the library when they see what you have started. We weren't surprised to find that everyone from students to faculty and community patrons enjoy working on these puzzles. The Library Student Advisory Board club has a little sign nearby reading, "Take some time and relax, compliments of the Library Student Advisory Board."

By our fifth year the puzzles were such a hit that we decided to host a game night for the puzzlers and video gamers. For our traditional gamers we have two teams of four or five students and two puzzles of 500 pieces. Each of the puzzles were similar in color and description. Teams were given sixty minutes to finish the puzzle and whichever team finished first won a prize. We also had our "Halo/Xbox 360 Game Craze" for video gamers on the same night. With the help of our audio-visual technician, our library club will be setting up four televisions with four controllers at each, allowing sixteen students to play at one time. Because our library will be open extra hours in the evening for this event, we have decided to combine both types of gaming. You could expand on this idea with checkers, chess, or other popular games. (Another suggestion we have received was to host a student chess competition.)

Library Open House

Each semester the library hosts an open house. Open to everyone, it targets students enrolled in the mandatory first-year seminar course. The aim of the open house is to reduce new-student anxiety about the library

Teresa Arthur, criminal justice/business law major and member of the LSAB, helping out at the library's open house.

and orient them to the collections and services the library offers.[1] Many students are required to attend this event. While most just go with the flow, a few let their true feelings be known. Some valuable, honest feedback received from club members who were required to participate was that we needed to integrate a bit more content into the event to make it seem "worth your while," even though the event is intended to let students explore the library and meet the staff in a fun, relaxed way.

Many Library Student Advisory Board members are sophomores or upper-division students, so they have some experience with faculty research expectations and the library. One year we had club members help with the revision and planning of the event, including a new theme: Treasure Island. The club also donated some of its funds, which the library matched, to purchase supplies, decorations, and give-aways for the open house. Event planners, including library staff, had a great time learning piratespeak and making decorations for the event.

Running the open house while still offering the full range of the library's services has proven to be a challenge to our small library staff. When we asked club members to donate their time on the day of the event, several readily agreed. Some helped

The Library Student Advisory Board even helped decorate the outside of the library for our open house.

with setup and teardown before and after the open house. Others staffed "stations" around the library, providing information and insight to visitors. A number of visitors commented that they liked the fact that other students were involved with the event. And more than once we overheard visitors ask a club member if they would *really* need to use the library in college. (The answer was yes.) We think that makes this partnership a huge success.

The following year the Library Student Advisory Board donated funds to rent a popcorn machine and associated supplies. The students loved this idea and the tantalizing smell brought everyone down to see what was going on in the library. The club also purchased karaoke CDs which helped pass the time for students waiting outside the library for their turn in the open-house treasure hunt. The students enjoyed showing off their talents and this also attracted others to come find out what was going on. We find that each of our new members bring more new ideas, helping the club and the library continue to grow.

User Satisfaction Survey

Recently club members suggested a survey to find out what users think about the library. Are they happy with the service? Did the library have the materials they were looking for? If we did, were they able to locate them? Are they happy with the library and its programs? Do they feel welcome upon entering your library? Do they find the atmosphere hospitable? Do they feel comfortable asking for the help they need? Are they happy with the hours of operation? The students felt that if we wanted the library to continue to grow, we needed to do this to find out what our patrons are thinking.

We thought this survey would be better received if it came from the club, so they worked on developing a survey. The club advisor sat down with members and discussed just what it was that we all wanted to learn in order to develop the questions to get the answers we were looking for. The club feels that the only way to keep our library usage elevated is to make sure we have what the patrons desire. With this in mind they put an open comment box at the end of the survey to let our patrons give suggestions for improving the library that none of us may have thought of before. However, due to issues surrounding how the survey will be distributed and collected, the club has put this idea on the back burner for the time being. See Appendix C for the survey developed by the Library Student Advisory Board.

If you do a satisfaction survey with your club, have club members distribute and tabulate the results. Surely one of them has learned how to make some nice graphs using the data collected. Distribute the survey to your library patrons, but also consider working with faculty to distribute the survey to students in their classes. You may even wish to have your faculty and staff on campus fill them out and see what comments they may have for you. When the results are tabulated, have the club discuss the results and develop a few suggestions for ways to improve, if needed, in areas receiving a low score. Then present the results to the library administration to discuss what is being done right in areas where the library received high marks and how the library can improve in areas that may have received low marks. Remember to check if your campus has any policies regarding the distribution of such a survey before proceeding.

READ Posters

As mentioned earlier, the Library Student Advisory Board has created numerous READ posters over recent years — more than forty altogether. The club purchased software available from the American Library Association to create their posters. In the posters the club has featured faculty and student authors, as well as campus faculty, staff, and students with their favorite books. Club members create the posters and our preservation department has been kind enough to print large, poster-size copies of the finished product for us. Posters are displayed in the library and around campus. We have offered "your face on a READ poster" prizes in raffles — and are a little surprised that students find this so appealing. Faculty often request copies of their poster for their own use. The disadvantage of using this software is that some knowledge of image-editing software, such as Adobe Photoshop, is required. However, we are certain you will be able to learn. Plus, it is likely that one or more of your students will already know how to use this software — and perhaps they can teach you a few new things about it too.

Printers

Students place a high value on their printing capabilities. In one instance, the club decided to use its funds to purchase a small color printer to print posters, flyers, bookmarks, and other club publications. The club and the library came to an agreement regarding this printer: library staff would have access to it in exchange for supplying ink cartridges and paper.

In another instance, the library's one and only public printer died at one of the busiest times of the semester. Although there were other printing options on campus, already stressed students became quite upset over this. As a result club leaders took it upon themselves to advocate on behalf of their peers and explain to administration just how badly this printer needed to be replaced quickly, and not haphazardly repaired again only to break down again in a few days. The bold action had the desired effect and a new printer made an appearance within a few days.

Library display case featuring the Library Student Advisory Board. Includes books and DVDs the LSAB purchased for the library, information about the club and the club's awards.

In Memoriam Donations

"When my (Marianne's) mother, Ann Snyder, passed away in the fall of 2006, the club wanted to honor her by donating something in her name to the library. My mother worked in the library as interlibrary loan assistant for many years before retiring. She was an avid library club member. The students adored her and I was very touched by this gesture by the club members. They have often heard us telling amusing stories of my mother and one of them was her frequent-asking for an umbrella stand for the library patrons. The students decided that this was what they wanted to purchase in her memory. After much searching, they bought a beautiful, oriental-style umbrella stand which now sits near the circulation desk with a name plate in honor of her many faithful years working at the library."

Displays

Creative displays can be a wonderful way to pique people's interests. Our library club tries to do a display on a new topic each month in one of the library's display

The Library Student Advisory Board entered a History Channel contest. To enter you had to submit a photo of your display on Franklin D. Roosevelt. The club worked very hard on this and even though they did not win they did receive the complete DVD set on FDR for the library's collections.

cases. These will often be related to celebrations, such as Women's History Month, Banned Books Week, Martin Luther King, Jr. Day, or Earth Day. As the club's interests have expanded, these displays are now more often related to their outside activities, such as a display on salsa dancing and Latino culture in preparation for the salsa dance they were planning.

During the summer months we usually put in two displays, one on the Library Student Advisory Board and how we support the library and give to the campus community. In the second case we display loaned Penn State paraphernalia from the campus bookstore. This gives visiting students and their parents a small glimpse of what the bookstore sells. The bookstore has been generous to the club and the library, so we like to return the favor.

Activities Contributing to the Campus

Activities contributing to the library contribute to the campus by extension. However, some of the club's efforts contribute more to the campus community than the library. The result of these activities are more students using the library and students acting as positive representatives of the library and the club, effectively advocating library use. Even though the popular DVDs and best sellers directly enhance library collections, we put them in this category because these materials bring in so many students who may not have used the library otherwise. And, in a region with very limited entertainment options for underage students, these popular items have helped improve the campus experience for our students.

Entertainment — Leisure Reading and Movies

Survey the campus environment and find out what the students' needs are. On our campus about a quarter of the student population lives on campus. Virtually all of these students come in with no ties to the community and often go home on the weekends until they make new friends and find things to do in the area. Most of them also come from large urban areas, a stark contrast to our campus's comparatively rural location. These students, in particular, were in need of evening and weekend leisure activities.

One of the club's first initiatives was to use some of their funds to purchase best sellers and DVDs to donate to the library. The library's mission is to support the academic needs of the students and there is rarely money to buy popular novels and movies. The items the club donates to the library are popular with all the students, and with students who live on campus in particular. And the display of new books and DVDs is now part of most library tours for new and prospective students. These items have helped increase our circulation and the total number of undergraduates registered at the library. But more importantly, they get students into the library and they start to see the other things we have to offer.

Video Games

One our club's newest initiatives is hosting a video-game console for students to use in the library. After considering the merits and popularity of the Microsoft Xbox 360, Nintendo Wii, and Sony Playstation II, the club decided to purchase the Wii console. The package included the console, controllers, memory, and five games. After discussing with the library staff how this might be offered to students, we went with the current model that we use for the laptops we circulate to students — two-hour in-house use only. Additionally, we barcoded each piece and placed them in a foam-core case. Club members decided that two hours was preferable to a three- or seven-day checkout, preventing one student from having the console for an extended period of time. One of our two study rooms equipped with a television is large enough for a few students to use the interactive game controllers. And, like the popular novels and DVDs, it gets the students into the library. See Appendix D for a sample Wii loan authorization form for use when students borrow the console.

The idea of purchasing a gaming console for student use was brought to the heads of the library for permission and was positively received. The next stop was for the club members to vote on which game console they wanted to purchase. A good deal of research was done on all consoles and it was decided to purchase the Nintendo Wii. After a very successful fund-raiser, our library club purchased the Wii shortly after the system was released and within a few weeks it was ours. The next step was barcoding for checkout, building a case, and securing the equipment with security labels. Bear in mind when you have something of value that you want to protect it. Have a list of rules and regulations for use of the gaming system so that everyone has an opportunity to enjoy it for a long time. Make this list as brief as possible. Make sure all your library staff, including student workers, receive proper training on the checkout and check-in procedures for all equipment. Last but not least: get the word out that your library now has a game console for student use. This was definitely the easiest part for us to do. The Wii had just arrived in the morning and by lunchtime we had students wanting to check it out. Word of mouth spreads fast and carries far. You will still want to put up flyers announcing your new item and the requirements for checking it out. Since making the Wii available it has been in use almost continuously. The library has enough rooms for studying that so far we haven't received any complaints about students using the room to play games. Likewise, we haven't had any complaints about noise.

Since the idea for the club to purchase a video-game console was first suggested, there has been the intention for the club and the library to host a game night for students. The Nintendo Wii was popular, but about a year after purchasing the Wii the club decided to also purchase a Microsoft Xbox 360 console to meet student demand. Once the club secured enough controllers for a large group to play, game night become a reality. Game night was held in the library after the library closed to avoid disturbing students who might be trying to concentrate. Since this was held after hours, the club advisor had to be there to open the building for gamers and supervise the event. We thought it was a great suggestion to open the game night to traditional gamers, too, and also sponsor a puzzle competition. We had a great turnout for game night and students really seemed to enjoy it. It is definitely something the club would like to do again.

Dances

In our fourth year as a club there were a few students who suggested hosting a dance. Having a dance is an exciting way to make friends, raise money, and introduce the library club to the rest of the campus community. Once we decided to start taking action on this idea, the first problem we had was deciding when to hold it. Since we are largely a commuter campus, sometimes we have trouble getting students to attend evening or weekend events because of scheduling conflicts with other events on campus (such as sporting events), students' work schedules, and the fact that many of our students go home for the weekend.

Nevertheless, we did not discourage them. We explained the problems and the responsibilities of holding dances on campus. To build support, the first thing they decided to do was to go out on campus and find out if other students wanted a dance. They also polled students about what time in the semester and day of the week was best for the dance, what kind of music they wanted to hear, and whether they wanted it to be casual or semi-formal. By the next meeting they had their answers and were ready to try to sell their idea to the rest of the club. The club members listened to what the students had to say and we ended the discussion with a vote. Because the students who wanted the dance came prepared with information and did a splendid job showing their research and enthusiasm, the dance was approved by everyone. This event is an attempt to improve the overall sense of community on campus by trying to get both commuters and on-campus students involved in the event.

Once the club voted yes, they had to then take it to the student affairs office for its permission and get all the information on policies for holding dances on university grounds. The club wanted to put on this dance with as little expense as possible, so they got as many in-house volunteers for the event as possible. They asked the campus audio-visual manager, who also happens to be the club co-advisor, if he would do the setup and act as DJ for the dance. For a small "fee" (a cheese pizza), he agreed. The club members took their favorite music and made their own CDs for the DJ to play, again costing the club nothing but their own time. Making our own decorations also only cost us time since each club receives a small supplies budget at the beginning of every year, which we use to make our posters, flyers, and decorations. We were not permitted to charge for admission to the dance, but student affairs did give us an additional $500 to purchase DVDs that semester.

The library club came up with a Mardi Gras theme for the dance. To promote the dance, club members handed out colorful flyers on campus and the library staff handed them out to all library patrons. On the evening of the dance, student club members decorated the cafeteria with Mardi Gras balloons and other colorful decorations. The club purchased inexpensive Mardi Gras beads online and handed out a necklace to everyone who came to the dance. The dance was a huge success, well-attended by both commuter and on-campus students.

After this dance, the club immediately started talking about having another dance again soon. One idea for the next dance was to invite the campus's step team to perform — a great way to work together with other clubs. Another idea was to work with the student affairs department to secure funding to bring in a live band for a dance. However, because the funding for the salsa band came from the pot created by the mandatory student activity fee, this dance couldn't be a fund-raiser for the club. Like the Mardi Gras dance, it had to be another "get to know you" dance. Despite this, the Library Student Advisory Board decided to hold a salsa dance in the fall with the aid of our student affairs department to secure the performers. Before the upcoming event the club created displays on salsa dancing and Latino culture for the library.

Local Restaurant Menus

During one of our brainstorming sessions one of our club members came up with the great idea of having a menu book. We have many students who are not familiar with the area and have no idea what restaurants are in our town. We thought this was a very clever idea and now the menu book is used all the time here in the library. Because we live in a small community the menus are not advertised in the local phone directory, and typically aren't available online. To create the menu book all the local students went out to their favorite restaurants and asked for takeout menus. They even tried to compete to see who could produce the most. While on their hunt they also kept in mind that some of these students would need places that delivered or restaurants close enough for people to walk safely. After we compiled our list and alphabetized it we put it into a 3-ring binder and got the word out to the students. This menu book has been used over and over again — and not only by students, but by staff and faculty alike. This menu book created a whole new outlook on the campus for several local restaurants, who were discovering this potential market for the first time. When the restaurants found out about our idea they offered coupons to their establishments for the students and even let us know of part-time job openings. You might be surprised at how your little club can open up the lines of communication. Just from starting a little menu file we have made friends with community members who now support our campus in a whole new way. They let us advertise our fund-raisers, put posters up for our annual car wash, and donate to our causes.

Dance Marathon

Since 1973 Penn State University students have been raising money for pediatric cancer research by holding a dance marathon. Raising over $51 million for the Four Diamonds Fund, "THON" is purportedly the largest student-run philanthropy in the world. When word got out that one of our club members had been affected by pediatric cancer the club decided to get involved. Earlier you read Loni's reflection about how her twelve-year-old nephew was diagnosed with lymphoma; he succumbed to the disease less than a year later. In accordance with the notion that keeping initiatives relevant to student member's interests keeps students involved with the club, members started raising money to support Loni as one of the dancers representing our campus.

You may ask what this has to do with the library. We did. But there are two reasons the club pursued this. The first is that student affairs encouraged the Library Student Advisory Board to do this because they have become known as the club that gets things done. Under Marianne's leadership as advisor, they knew that the necessary money, and more, would be raised. The second reason is that this campus- and university-wide exposure would raise awareness about the club and its activities among the student population and even in the wider community.

Book Club

Library Student Advisory Board members sponsor an informal student- and staff-run book club. Selections are of student and staff choice and the club is open to anyone interested, both on campus and in the local community. This is a great opportunity for resident students to meet commuter students and find people with similar interests in the local area. It is also a wonderful way for local community members to spend some time on campus and find out more about our students. It was decided that the club would meet twice a month during the noon hour. The first book selected was *True Believer* by Nicholas Sparks.

This title was selected because we wanted an easy read for the end of the semester. Also, its perceptions and realities of living in both a small town and a large city reflect the types of discussions that happen daily on our campus. This aspect of the book sparked quite an interesting discussion among a diverse group of faculty, staff, students, and community members. We didn't really think we could get students interested in a book club, but it does seem that the interest is there and we are looking forward to planning more book club meetings with the LSAB in the future.

Carnival

We encourage our club members to recruit whenever and wherever possible, year-round. We are always trying to persuade new students to join our club and help support the library. At the end of every spring semester our student affairs department hosts a themed carnival. The carnival starts around noon, offering a barbeque lunch and serving treats like Italian ice and cotton candy. They always have a DJ playing popular hits and games set up not only for the students' amusement, but also for staff and faculty. Everybody comes together for these fun-filled events — it's a great stress reliever and a nice way to end the semester and the school year.

We have found that this is also a good opportunity to get a jump start on recruiting new members for next fall. While casually talking at the carnival about plans for

A great place to recruit new club members is the annual Spring Carnival, which is held by the Student Affairs Department.

145

Dr. Michael Gallis (left), associate professor of physics, and LSAB member Jonathan Seiler, history major, competing at the Spring Carnival.

the summer and what courses they will be talking in the fall, our club members somehow managed to recruit new club members to join them at meetings in the fall. Often students will bring new recruits over to introduce them to Marianne, and she makes sure to get their names and e-mail addresses so she can add them to her e-mail list and keep in touch with them about the club over the summer.

Activities Contributing to the Community

Moved by the unfortunate circumstance of others, in recent years the club has decided to use some of their time and money to give back to the community and those in need. The devastation of Hurricane Katrina was quickly followed by devastation closer to home, getting the club involved in the fight to find a cure for cancer. As described above and earlier in this book, club members became involved in the PSU "THON" dance marathon event and fund-raiser that not only changed their lives and their sense of campus community, but also contributed to the $5–6 million raised each year to support pediatric cancer research and families of children with cancer. On a lighter note, the club can also contribute to their local community by welcoming the community to events on campus and in the library. These events can serve to help build the "town and gown" relationship, or perhaps even become fund-raising events.

Donation to Charities

Following the devastation to New Orleans and the Gulf Coast caused by Hurricane Katrina, club members donated $50 to the Red Cross — the club's first charity donation — earmarked for hurricane victim relief efforts. A few years later the Library Student Advisory Board got involved with the United Way and participated in a "Tug-a-Bug" event held on campus. In an amazing feat of strength, the club kids outmaneuvered the women's basketball team and showed the best time for a sprint down the campus pedestrian mall with a Volkswagen Beetle in tow. For this feat, $5,000 was donated to the United Way in the name of the Library Student Advisory Board. Finally, when the family of the club's president lost their house to a fire, the Library Student Advisory Board joined other groups on campus in raising funds for this family, donating $200 to the campus fund to help this family get back on their feet.

Local Recipe Book

When the library club started to earn their own money (unrestricted funds) they wanted to be able to help others outside the campus community. It started with Hurricane Katrina, as described above. Shortly thereafter we found out that our club's vice president, Loni Picarella, had a young cousin, Nathan McFadden, with lymphoma. Our club became involved with Nathan and his family. Club members sent Nathan cards and they gave him a Penn State T-shirt and stadium blanket. They also kept Nathan and his family in their thoughts and prayers. Nathan fought his cancer for nearly a year before he died. We were devastated. That is when we decided to become involved with Penn State THON. We wanted to help fight pediatric cancer. We went "canning" to raise money, and also donated $200 of our own money. Loni and a partner were selected by the campus to represent Penn State Schuylkill at the 48-hour, no-sitting, no-sleeping dance marathon. We all supported her. During this time we were not just a club, we were a family. Read more about how important this was to her in chapter 2, in her reflections on the personal benefits of club membership.

The next year Loni became the LSAB president and came to the club again for support. The American Cancer Society was working on a cookbook for Nathan called *Nate's Mates: Heavenly Recipes* and Loni needed everyone's favorite recipes to contribute to the cookbook. The club members were thrilled to be able to help again.

Once the cookbook was finished the students helped the McFadden family sell them for the American Cancer Society.

Art Displays

Bring in your local artists and artisans for displays of their works. Turn your library into an art gallery. Have fun with it and use your imagination. This is something our library has done in the past and would like to try again with input from the club. If you would like to try this, get your students involved by asking the students about the kinds of art they are interested in or if they know any local artists. Perhaps you will want to start small with a single artist's display and work your way up to an evening or weekend art show. You could also have artists do a demonstration.

Look for local art talent in your community. Call upon any friends who are artists, or talk with your art faculty about their work and local artists they might recommend for the event. Or, contact your local arts organizations. If you do decide to host an art exhibit, do be sure that you have a display case that can be locked. When you are bringing in someone's work you want to be able to assure them that their art work will be properly secured.

An art teacher at one of our local high schools creates amazing pottery. He digs his own clay, uses a potter's wheel to make his creations, and bakes the clay in a hillside kiln. We contacted him to see if he would be interested in doing a display in our library. He was flattered and we were honored that he consented. He brought in his works and we provided a description of the type of clay and baking that he does. We also incorporated our library books on pottery into the display. We then let the campus community know through e-mail and flyers about this exciting opportunity. We kept the display up for a month so that there was time for everyone on- and off-campus to visit. Since he is well-known in the community, the library had hordes of people coming to see this artist's creations. This was a great opportunity for the library to get in some new visitors, and the art teacher was pleased because people asked if his pottery could be purchased.

Another route would be to contact your local high schools about talented students. Invite the students to bring a piece of their work to be displayed, whether it be a painting, mosaic tiles, jewelry, or pottery. Host an evening for the students and their parents to visit the library and see everyone's work. This is a way to bring in students that are thinking about going to college onto your campus, an event campus administration will surely be interested in attending. Give them an opportunity to see what your campus can offer them. Invite the art professors of your campus to attend, or perhaps even to speak.

On a large scale, think about gathering the local artists for a "Sidewalk Art

Show." However, make sure you have a rain date or inside location on reserve in the event of bad weather. Set up tables and chairs outside and decorate with signs and balloons. Put laminated nameplates on the tables introducing each participating local artist and include a little biography. Let them display and sell their wares. If you can get another club or your student affairs department involved, they may be able to supply food and music. Although this is not in the library, be sure that people know the event was arranged by the student library club. And consider having refreshments or special exhibits in the library to draw the crowd into the library.

Other possibilities include a music festival to showcase student talents, local bands, or an open mike night. Our club sponsored an event billed as an open mike night, but which also falls into the category of "poetry slam." Students got together in the library to express their feelings through their own poetry or read their favorite author's poems. The library club students arranged and advertised the event and provided refreshments for the entertainers and their audience. You and your club members can have a lot of fun featuring students and community members' talents — and at little or no expense to the club. Be sure that the community is aware of these events and know that they are welcome to attend. And don't forget to explore the possibility of using these events as fund-raisers.

Working with the Library and the Campus

Build Members' Relationships with Library Directors and Staff

Just because library administration and staff are supportive of the concept of a library club does not mean they will be accepting and supportive of all the club's suggestions and ideas. Sometimes you, as advisor, will need to act as the bridge between the library staff and the club. Either side may have difficulty explaining their rationale for proposing or dismissing an idea, but as someone who understands both sides, you can act as interpreter and encourage further discussion to find a compromise.

Your Job as Interpreter

You may find yourself surprised by how many innovative ideas enthusiastic club members will come up with. Not every idea will work for your library, but do not let an idea from left field be immediately dismissed just because something like it has never been done before. Club members will quickly become discouraged and fade away if they feel their suggestions and ideas are not taken seriously. A suggestion to host a night for students who are enthusiastic video gamers did not initially receive a warm welcome from library administration, though some public and academic libraries have already ventured into this realm. However, over time the same idea kept resurfacing, building support for the notion that this is something the students would really like and that the library would be a good host for such an event. As discussed earlier, the club has since raised the funds to purchase both Nintendo Wii and Microsoft Xbox 360 game consoles, controllers, and games for student use in the library. We have even hosted a game night featuring both old-school jigsaw puzzles and video games.

Encourage Open Doors

If your library administration is willing to keep open dialogue with students, encourage club members to stop by to share ideas with other library faculty and staff members, just as they do with you. Some student ideas may have big implications for circulation, acquisitions, cataloging, or reference staff. For example, books donated to the library by the club each receive a bookplate, as well as the regular cataloging and labeling that needs to be done. But as long as donations are in small batches, it should not significantly affect the workflow of any staff members processing items. A challenge we used to face was helping students find the videos donated by the club in the library's collection. Keeping with traditional library organization, our videos are LC-classed and, until recently, were shelved with the books and other materials in the general circulating collection. However, browsing the video selection using the library's catalog is not quite the same as browsing the shelves in a video store. To make the popular videos easier to browse, we started maintaining a binder containing a sheet describing each video. Reminiscent of browsing the shelves in the video store, the sheets are filed according to genre — such as action, comedy, or drama — with the new releases and recently arrived in the front. Of course we are all very grateful for the club's donations, but it does create some additional work to maintain this book. Recently, with a bit of influence from the club and library staff, the head librarian decided to create a separate location for the video collection, making the titles easier both to search and to browse. This change, reducing confusion about searching and locating videos, has resulted in a drastic increase in use of the video collection.

When club members and library staff work together to develop a plan that works for everyone, it benefits the students without overextending library staff. We think you will find that as the library staff come to know the club members and see that they are truly interested in making the library a better place — a place to which all students will want to come — they will become more willing to work with the students to realize their ideas. In our case, resistance or disinterest on behalf of the staff has not been an issue. They have been on board since day one and have provided a great support network.

Another way to build the club's relationship with the library administration and staff is to invite them to meetings. This way the library can participate in brainstorming sessions, developing sound, well-rounded, easy-to-implement ideas to which everyone contributed. However, it should be clear that this is a brainstorming session in which there are no bad ideas that can be immediately dismissed. Sometimes students will have great ideas, but even they have difficulty expressing how the library will benefit. As advisor, take the opportunity to bridge the gap and encourage everyone to explore the full potential of each idea. For example, when club members suggested developing a film browsing collection arranged like the video stores students are familiar with, library administration initially resisted. However, through discussion a compromise was reached and a small collection of "recently arrived" videos for students to browse was created near the notebooks we maintain for browsing by genre. Further discussion and consideration led to the decision to relocate the entire video collection to a highly visible location for even easier browsing.

However, you may find the presence of outsiders to be a hindrance to effective brainstorming. As alluded to by former LSAB president Ashley Fehr in her reflection, students may find the presence of library or campus administration at the meeting a bit intimidating. In this case, you may find it more productive to have club officers make a special presentation to library policy makers of well-formed ideas for improving the library as a student space or for changing existing policies to better accommodate student needs, along with a plan for implementing the ideas.

Student Reflection on Developing Relationships with Campus Administration

Past LSAB president Ashley Fehr shares her thoughts below on working with a new campus administrator. We had a new chancellor at our campus and tensions were running a bit high as we waited to learn our new leader's plans for campus. Like Patrick Troutman, Ashley was also an enthusiastic club leader. Her dedication and let's-get-it-done attitude helped the club achieve many things during her tenure in the club's early years. Ashley graduated in 2008 with honors, earning a bachelor's degree in English.

Best Friends
by Ashley Fehr

In college, administrators carry intimidating titles and presence. "Provost" means "the keeper of a prison," hardly a welcoming thought. To an incoming college frosh, these people lurk in distant offices, making policies and occasionally surfacing to make a speech. But the connection between the administration and students requires more than just signatures.

As the LSAB president, I found myself facing these names and policies many times. Most events that we planned or ideas we had ended up on an administrator's desk at one point, and sometimes more than once. The system can be frustrating at times, but the longer the club exists, the easier it is to operate within the boundaries and become familiar with the proceedings. Our yearly events, especially fund-raisers, proved most efficient due to experience.

Planning time for special events is our most prolific time for ideas, as these provide a chance to work on something new. These are also times when the administration is most involved and aware of our activities. Ciletti Library's tenth anniversary was to be celebrated with alumni, benefactors, students, and faculty. The ceremony would reflect not only the library, but the university as a whole.

The anniversary coincided nicely with Arbor Day. We decided to celebrate both and commemorate the anniversary by planting trees. Ideas were tossed around regarding type and location — flowering dogwood next to the walkway, a tree named after a Russian princess by the bench, a crab apple right in the middle of the lawn. We thought we had things decided — and then we met the campus master plan which did not match our own. So began a long chain of communication with the administration, discussing not only trees but all aspects of the ceremony. Like many club members, I was sending e-mails between classes, dropping by the administration building on lunch hours, and making phone calls to Mari on the weekends in anticipation of the event. Unrestricted flow of communication is vital to the well-being of the club. Members that are constantly aware of happenings are more likely to be involved.

The tree planting idea drew mixed response. Some administrators immediately liked the idea whereas others felt the hassle wasn't worth it. However, after many meetings, e-mails, and phone calls, enough administration backed us and the trees were planted.

Another key aspect of the anniversary celebration was that LSAB members were present in the library the entire day, providing tours and information. I feel that the public was pleased to see so many students actively engaged and enthusiastic about the library. One of our now former presidents, Patrick Troutman, also spoke at the engagement.

The need for communication is also reflected university-wide. As in any business atmosphere, there is a certain level of speculation surrounding the university faculty members. Most students hear about administration members prior to meeting them. My own expectations were shaped this way. Our university reorganized and we received a new chancellor. Reorganization stirred panic in the LSAB. Would we lose funding? Already operating with a limited budget, losing any more monetary support would severely cripple the efforts of the club. With a lot of uncertainties, we were eager to meet with administration and find out our fate.

Sitting in Marianne's office one afternoon, I interrupted her work and asked for her opinion of the chancellor. I trusted Mari to tell me if we had a friend or foe sitting in the A-building.

"He seems like he cares," Mari eagerly said. Excellent. Let's go see what we can work out.

As I was exiting class one morning, the new chancellor was in the hallway, about to enter a luncheon retirement party. I debated breezing right by him to get a forty-five-cent coffee in the library, and then remembered Mari's description.

"Hello. You're the new Chancellor, right? I want to introduce myself."

The job of the president in any organization is never easy. I put my coffee on hold despite my veins longing for it. I could no longer stand the mystery; I had to know for myself if I would spend the next few months whining about this guy. Automatically, my hand leapt forward to meet his, bright smile on, hoping for the best.

Luckily, the chancellor was willing to risk missing out on apple pie to get acquainted. After quick introductions and promises for future conversations, we parted ways.

I bolted as quickly as my un-caffeinated self could, back to the library, burst through the staff door, breathless with excitement and announced "I just met the Chancellor."

The Library Student Advisory Board

Marianne spun around from her computer screen, pushed her bangs out of her eyes, and asked, "What do you mean you met the chancellor?"

Mari knows me well. She knows how I will react to a situation. She knows that if the chancellor offended me I would swear war on him or whine endlessly.

"Oh, we're best friends," I assured her. "I think it's going to be a good year." Having someone in office willing to work with students to promote general well-being on campus is priceless. Throughout my term as president, many events ran smoothly and successfully because we felt comfortable approaching the chancellor and administration with requests and questions.

The student-administration relationship depends on many factors. In large schools, deans may struggle to recognize more than a handful of students. That is why having a few chief "go to" people is so important. While the entire club needs to be supporting and active, a strong advisor and cabinet will be a determining factor in the success of the club.

While it is important for *everyone* to be recognized, these individuals should be the first wave in making contact with administration. As a former president, I realized that I had to sometimes step outside of my comfort zone and approach people.

Penn State Schuylkill's student affairs department helped to make this easier by having student organization members attend meetings and luncheons about campus proceedings. The LSAB and the Student Government Association collaborated on many events. Instead of vying to be the top organization on campus, there is a genuine interest in actually providing services to students. Clubs with the largest rosters are not necessarily the most efficient.

Collaborations with other organizations are not only vital to the well-being of the campus, but also to the welfare of your own group. Sharing the responsibility of hosting an event or fund-raiser often means more people to do what needs doing.

Being a club that is willing to reach out to the campus and community, the LSAB has worked on some interesting projects. My favorite event was the scholarship dinner for Mr. Beach. James Beach had retired many years before I enrolled at Penn State. Patty Schoener, alumni and development specialist, approached the club after seeing some of our other events. Vice president Loni Picarella and I spent countless hours trying to understand a man we had never met. Through reading old yearbooks, chorale albums, and talking to past students of his, we learned that we were facing the difficult task of portraying a beloved man.

Patty handed us the reins for the event, allowing the club to decide how we wanted to express the devotion and admiration that surrounded Mr. Beach. The project became archaeological, as we tried to reconstruct the past, piecing together a personality from filing cabinets and boxes stuffed with memorabilia. We made story boards that consisted of pictures, letters, sheet music, programs, and other artifacts.

After the scholarship dinner, I had the opportunity to meet Mr. Beach and his wife. We spent the afternoon in the library talking and he answered some of our questions about inside jokes. This project was my favorite because the outcome was so rewarding, knowing that we reminded many people of good times.

A lot of dinner guests were surprised to know we had that much memorabilia in the library which could be accessed at any time. I find one of the most surprising parts of working at the library is how many resources are unknown. As a frequent patron of the library, I didn't realize this at first. I think it is very vital for libraries to think like first-time patrons at all times. Something that seems obvious to us may not be so clear to others.

Libraries need advertising, too. Having a positive relationship with administration has helped our club to hold many successful events. Despite the titles, administration shouldn't be feared, but rather worked with.

Working with the Library

The activities of our Library Student Advisory Board have led to great contributions to our library. Their collection donations and the increase in library usage resulting in part from their efforts have a positive impact on the library, but could possibly have a negative effect on staff workflow if not managed properly. We hope you might find that any additional work created by the club's efforts will be offset by the improvement in morale when staff see their work is being appreciated by the club and the student body.

Implications for Reference and Instruction

Peak usage of the library in 2007 is up 112 percent over 2002. Peak usage in 2008 may even be higher. Comparing usage data from the fourth week in the semester in 2002 and 2007, usage is up 188 percent. We don't exactly know why, but believe it is partly, perhaps even largely, due to the club.

Each student coming in to borrow a DVD gives one of us the opportunity to show a student the print guide ("the book") for the DVD collection — which they usually preferred initially — but also to show them how to find videos in our online catalog by title or genre. Many, once they had exhausted the possibilities in our local collection, would start branching out to see what videos other campuses had for them to borrow. Later in the semester, when they needed a book for a research assignment, they were already comfortable asking us for help and many were already familiar with the catalog and requesting items from other campuses.

As students came in to return novels or videos and borrow more, they would engage us in conversations about what they had just read or watched: "Have you read this? What did you think? You should watch this." As the semester progressed, during our conversations some students would start commenting about the disappointing grade they got for using Wikipedia as a source, improperly citing their sources, or not citing their sources at all — the perfect opportunity to say, "Next time, come see us first. We can help you with that." For some of them, library instruction had already been provided in their class, sometimes more than once, but it didn't always register if the instruction did not have an immediate application. We also hear an alarming number of students say that they were encouraged to use Internet sources such as Wikipedia in high school, making our library instruction even less relevant.

If you are open to critique, ask for club members' feedback on library activities, such as instructional workshops. Club members may offer constructive criticism, or at least offer suggestions when prompted. Club members helped us spread the word about library workshops more effectively in order to reach a wider audience. Also, timing is crucial when students are looking for "just in time" instruction, rather than "just in case." We had been offering the bulk of our library workshops at the beginning of the semester and repeating the most popular later in the semester, but for that "just in time" instruction, it seems like late October and November are preferred.

When it comes to events on our campus, the holy grail of advertising is the personal daily organizer distributed to students each year. Campus events are listed in the organizer which many students adopt for their personal use, but this requires planning events nearly a year in advance. We found that by getting our events in the organizer we could get the word out to more students, but that our workshops almost always ended up conflicting with other events and that spreading the word about changed date, time, or location of an advertised event was very difficult. So, we polled our club members about the best way to let them know about library workshops, and were surprised when many recommended e-mail. They recommend sending an e-mail to all students about library workshops at the beginning of the semester, and a reminder a day or two before each workshop. Feeling overwhelmed by e-mail ourselves, we were afraid that students would simply delete these messages, but we tried it and it seems there is a bit of improvement in attendance. We send an e-mail with a schedule of the library's workshops and a link to more information on the library's Web site at the beginning of the semester, and then arrange for our events to be included on the weekly message sent to students about upcoming events and activities on campus. Prior to this we had been advertising workshops on our library's homepage (students primarily access library resources through the umbrella university libraries Web site for all campuses and don't realize there is a campus library Web site with campus-specific information such as this), on the online campus events calendar (which we doubt many students use), and through the First-Year Seminar course. Advertising through this course is still most effective because there is faculty endorsement of the workshops and many of these students are required to attend a set number of campus events for class. However, this reaches a narrow segment of the campus population.

Another implication of student involvement with reference and instruction activities lies in the influence the Library Student Advisory Board members had on improving the appeal and student-centeredness of library programs, especially the library's open house. In order to incorporate club members' ideas into the planning, we got feedback immediately after the fall and spring open-house events. Rather than waiting until the quiet summer months to start planning the next fall open house, we got a jump start on the planning process and started to work on plans with the club before the students left for the summer. Many of the details were worked out over the summer, but student input on the theme and activities to incorporate in the open house was solicited in the spring. Then, when club members returned in fall, volunteers from the club were requested to help prepare for and execute the event. Students helped prepare signage, decorated, staffed information and entertainment stations during the event, and helped take down and store signs and decorations for next year. Their input helped make the event more appealing to students, but also greatly contributed to what we were able to accomplish by doubling, perhaps even tripling the number of staff.

Ultimately, the implications for reference and instruction from the increase in library use due to club activities are simply more reference questions and one-on-one instruction requests. Of course, to catch them all, to take advantage of each situation to market your services as it presents itself, we really had to be in the right place at the right time. I am sure there were opportunities that were missed, but we were also able to take advantage of many opportunities. And as a result of club members' input, we were able to improve the student-centeredness and appeal of our library programs, such as our library open house.

Use the opportunity to get input from students — and the "student perspective" may vary from one individual to the next — but be careful not to let the club develop a sense that they are the ones running the library. Student perspective matters, but it has to be taken and applied to the larger context of the library's position within the university. Taking the time to share this perspective with club members will help students see where their avenues for influence exist. Don't discourage the enthusiasm generated when students see they have the power to create change, but give them an occasional glimpse at the boundaries.

Implications for Staff

Implications for staff stemming from Library Student Advisory Board activities are insignificant, according to library staff member Rosanne Chesakis. Possible increased workload from club donations of books, DVD, and items such as video games and game consoles has proven to be negligible, as they are really no different from any other donation to the library. Indeed, these donations are more predictable than most and have already been approved by the head librarian to be added to the collection. Even the challenge of barcoding the Wii and getting it ready to circulate like a reserve item was taken in stride.

Additionally, time away from regular duties to attend club meetings in order to act as a sounding board for club ideas has not proven to have a significant impact on the staff. Indeed, increased interaction with students helps members of the staff—especially those who work behind the scenes and interact little, if at all, with the student body—to develop a connection with students and a better understanding of student life. Indeed, they may even come to feel like a privileged insider, at least among a segment of the student population. According to Rosanne, the ability to get to know more of our students has even led to a "nicer work environment."

In addition, we have found that when library student workers are also members of the club, they develop a better understanding of the library and become better at their jobs. Perhaps they feel a stronger connection to the library and its goals. Student employees who are also club members seem to care a little bit more. But Rosanne has also noticed a blurring of the boundaries between employment at the library and membership in the club. All student employees are invited and encouraged to become members of the Library Student Advisory Board, and many of them do join. Indeed, it is becoming increasingly difficult to ensure that the circulation desk is staffed during the club's meeting time. But sometimes student employees assume all club members are library employees and there has been some accidental merging of club and student employee business. For example, student employees have unwittingly invited non-employees to employee training and recognition events, think this was just like any other club meeting. Our current club president, who also happens to be a library student employee, has suggested the club start an employee-of-the-month recognition program. Though this might seem outside of the club's realm, he made the case to get it on the club's next agenda and convinced the group to recommend it to the library. In another example of the lines between the club and the library blurring, it is the library staff that decides the employee-of-the-month and an announcement is now made at each of the club's monthly meetings.

And perhaps this is how it should be. Student employees involved with the club often complete duties or assist with projects that save the regular staff time. But it is somewhat unclear whether these student workers ask for more work or suggest a project on their own, or if they are caught in the vicious cycle of good work rewarded with more work. Perhaps being involved with the club simply gives them a stronger sense of belonging, and thus a stronger sense of responsibility. However, from time to time, enthusiastic student workers or volunteer club members may seem like pests when you are trying to concentrate on your own work. Rather than let yourself get frustrated, put all that energy you wish *you* had to good use and give them a project to work on. A tedious job? Let them work in pairs. In your quiet moments, anticipate the arrival of eager students and prepare brief, clear, written instructions for them so you will be ready. Try to convey the importance of this project, the method, and the desired result. For large projects, have students log their progress for you so anyone can pick up where they left off.

Students proactive about learning their job duties can result in fewer scheduled trainings taking regular staff from their other duties. Student workers proactive about learning their job and asking questions when faced with a new challenge can also lead to fewer mistakes needing correction by the full-time staff. However, overconfidence can also lead to mistakes. And occasionally student workers and club members have felt that they were above the rules and extended themselves special privileges with loans of books, videos, and the library's loaner laptops. And occasionally they have also extended these privileges to their friends. When these problems occur, we are sure to quickly correct their misguided assumption. We reinforce this by demonstrating that the full-time staff is not above the library's rules either, being sure to check out materials to ourselves the proper way, not eat or take personal phone calls at the public service desk, and so on. And on a few occasions we have also had a few students who got too comfortable being in staff areas, to the point where they were becoming a nuisance to staff trying to work or students in the surrounding areas if they were too loud. Fortunately, they respond well to suggestions that they move on to a more appropriate space.

The benefits of club activities for regular library staff members seem to outweigh any negative implications, which seem to be largely nonexistent for us. The processing of LSAB donations to the library and time spent acting as a sounding board for student ideas both during and outside regular meeting times does not seem to have a large impact on our staff. Our club members donate about fifty items per semester. This isn't necessarily a large donation in the grand scheme of things. The pressure to prepare and process — catalog and mark — these items quickly for student use has not been a problem.

Knowing Your Limitations

We do not want to dampen anyone's enthusiasm or excitement about what the library club can accomplish in this section. With careful planning and hard work, we are sure your club can accomplish anything it sets out to do. But we do know from experience that there can be unforeseeable barriers in your club's journey to success — and getting around those roadblocks aren't always easy. It can take some time to find the right solution. Sometimes that solution is putting an idea on the back burner and talking with people to work out the issues. If the idea is one the club is passionate about, be persistent about working through the difficulties and come back to the idea when everyone is ready. With patience, the time will come.

Be Realistic About What Your Students Can Accomplish

Know your limitations. We all have great ideas sometimes. We get excited. We jot our ideas down on little pieces of paper and cannot wait to share our ideas with others. Then, bam! You get hit with, "No, I'm sorry that will not do, we do not really have the funds for that, [or enough time or enough help]." Sometimes you have to be realistic about what you and your club members can actually accomplish. Sometimes your ideas are just a little out of your reach. You need to realize that you only have so much time, money, and energy to spend on your club and your club's ideas.

However, keep a log book of your ideas, or at least be sure they're recorded in your meeting's minutes. Even though you cannot make them a reality at the time does not mean that you will not find the funding or support for them at a later date. When the idea of buying more popular magazines for students came up at our very first meeting, we did not have any money in our club account yet. Once we raised some funds we were able to make this one of the club's priorities. As advisor, along with my other records, I, Marianne, keep a folder (actually many folders) of ideas. I go over them with the group periodically to see if there are ideas we want to add to our goals for the year.

You also need to set limitations on the amount of time you, as advisor, will spend on club activities — and then stick to them. While working on getting the club started I have already put in twenty-four hours a week as the advisor for the Library Student Advisory Board. Not everyone can spare that kind of time. More importantly, you do not need to give that much time to have a prosperous club.

For those of you with little time left for club matters, make sure that you have good, competent student leaders who can spare time during the week to take a lot of the burden of paperwork and e-mails off your shoulders. Every year is different with your student club members, but I have found that each year we have a number of hardworking students in the club who are at the library every day. They are always more than willing to help you with the important tasks at hand. Remember that your student leaders should be carrying much of the burden. Be in touch with you them on a regular basis and remind them of their duties when necessary. Also, your coworkers can be a great help to you. Do not hesitate to ask for their assistance. Periodically send out "special thanks" e-mails to club members and coworkers and let them know how much you appreciate their help.

Benefits of Working with a Library Student Advisory Board

Amy's Story

I arrived at the Penn State Schuylkill campus just about the same time that Marianne and the library were deciding to start a library club. With my freshly minted Master of Science in Library and Information Science I was feeling a little overwhelmed by my new job, but was also primed and ready to accept any new ideas. I had a history with the university, both as an undergraduate and a library staff member, but no history at Schuylkill to cloud my thoughts about the group's potential. I also lacked experience at a small university campus. My high school was bigger than this campus. I didn't yet realize that in such a place you really could get to know every student if you tried, though I had been told it was possible. I didn't yet realize that you really could get every one of them to use the library if you tried. I'm not saying we succeeded at this, but I do believe that it is possible.

When I first heard they planned to call the club the Library Student Advisory Board, I thought, "Okay, they'll *advise.*" Then I got confused when, from the very beginning, Marianne started talking about holding fund-raisers. And the more Marianne talked the more I began to see the similarities to the friends groups commonly found at public libraries in communities across the nation. In my mind, at least, public library friends groups — and LSAB — are more about the people than raising enormous amounts of money for special collections and endowments, as in traditional academic library friends groups. And of course the composition of LSAB is different — a group of students rather than prominent community members and bibliophilic faculty. The more I began to understand the vision, the more excited I got. Marianne was excited, and her excitement is contagious.

I am probably one of the people who benefited more from the club than I invested in it. Over the years, scheduling conflicts have prevented me from attending many of the club's meetings, but I would stop in when I could and would always catch up with Marianne later about the club's activities. Much of my collaboration with the club has been out of sheer necessity. When I needed a student's opinion, I asked the club. When I needed more help with the library open house, I asked the club. And they always responded.

If you've read the student reflections on the club, you may have noticed that the students sometimes see things differently from us. I was tempted to correct them when they didn't use quite the right library jargon to describe something. But it was more difficult not to react when I thought they weren't getting the right thing out of their experience with the club. For example, when Patrick expressed dismay about the lack of social activity at the library, "[students using] the library solely for research purposes and last-minute studying," a voice in the back of my head screamed, "But that's good! In fact, that is great!" If there are students in the library doing research and studying, what is the problem? But if the goal is to get *all* the students in the library — and if by "get all the students in the library" we mean get students to use collections and our services when needed — there are inevitably some students who need to be attracted by means other than our traditional virtues. Do other campus service providers aim for such an impossible usage rate? Popular DVDs, books, and video games are our version of sugary sweet snacks luring in passersby. Hearing those words, "Hey Amy, I have a paper due — can you help me?" from the student who came in daily for weeks to get a new movie or just to chat makes me feel great.

During the process of writing this book a great job opportunity appeared at another Penn State campus. As difficult a decision as it was to leave the Penn State Schuylkill campus, I decided that I could not pass up this opportunity. I miss the friends that I made there the most, but I also greatly miss the connection I had with the students at Schuylkill. Now I am considering starting a library student advisory board at my new campus, putting me in the same position as many of our readers. I suspect that as for many of you, finding the time to do this seems to be biggest hurdle. If you are wondering about this too, please continue reading through the epilogue of this book.

Fortunately Marianne and I realized that we were wrong to even question our former club members about their essays. The great thing about our club is that many students have gotten as much out of the club as they put in. And each student takes away something different. We hope this helps readers better understand the value of having students volunteer their time for the library.

10

Future of the Library Student Advisory Board

Evolution

The evolution of this extraordinary club has been astonishing. In the five short years since the club started we have gone from establishing a new club on campus by twisting the arms of eight unlikely students, to having a great relationship with a club of fifty-two active members that is ever expanding its reach on campus and in the community. Thinking back to the club's beginnings and seeing how much we all have all accomplished on our campus is overwhelming. What started out as a simple job as advisor has turned into a part-time occupation. And I love every minute of it. The library has gone from quiet stacks and empty study rooms to busy common rooms full of students alternating between being downright boisterous and shushing each other when it gets too loud. We now have students waiting in line to use our computers and the library is nearly as busy at 8:00 A.M. as at any other time of the day.

The Library Student Advisory Board started out by meeting once a month and giving helpful suggestions to promote the library in order to draw students in for much-needed reference help, and to make the library a welcoming place for all. The library club worked hard to get its name and reputation out to the student population and campus community in order to gain their attention and respect. We never dreamed that what started out as a simple idea for a little library club on our campus would turn into such an overwhelming success.

As we write this, the club's direction and activities of the Library Student Advisory Board's fifth year have evolved in such a way that sometimes we wonder where the library fits in anymore. But, we remind ourselves that hosting dances for the campus community increase awareness of the campus library and pushing ourselves out into the local community conveys a positive image of both the library and the campus to community members. On a few occasions these actions have even resulted in donations to the library — a result we would like to encourage. More faculty and staff are donating books, audio books, and DVDs to the library — both new and used — since they have become aware of the club and what it is trying to do. When alumni and community members discovered at the scholarship dinner honoring Mr. Beach that we had a collection of photographs and memorabilia documenting campus and community history, they started donating theirs to the library to add to our collection and be preserved in our archives. Plus, a local business regularly donates the soap, sponges, and other supplies needed for the Library Student Advisory Board's annual car wash. Maybe someday the club's actions will result in cash donations either to the library or even the club to help with its philanthropic activities. Perhaps we will even receive a sizeable donation.

When we are engaged in these events — and even when we are arranging them — we "sell" the library by sharing our view of the library as a great place to relax and spend time with friends, to get research and reference guidance, to come to the many library skills workshops offered, and to study quietly or meet with a group. Some of the new directions the club has taken this year include hosting a salsa dance, and participating in a United Way community fund-raiser event. Both events boosted the library's public image among the student body and in the local community.

Salsa Dance

In the spring of 2007, our club decided that it wanted to hold a salsa dance. It seemed like a bold move, but showed a lot of creativity. Members did their research and found numerous bands that would travel to our area, as there were no local salsa bands. For $2,500 a band would travel to from New York City to Pennsylvania, play for three hours, emcee the dance, and also offer free salsa lessons for students before the evening's festivities began. Their rate seemed quite pricey, but the club members wanted to give the students a night to remember! Members of the Library Student Advisory Board worked with the campus programming board and the student affairs department to coordinate the event. New on our campus this year, the programming board was implemented to coordinate all student events on campus. The programming board ensures that a balanced, diverse slate of entertainment and educational programs are offered each month. Centralized planning also helps eliminate overlapping events. The programming board meets once each month with a representative from all campus clubs to develop the campus events calendar. Student members are trained how to plan programs and make them successful, as well as how to be fiscally responsible and utilize all the resources on campus to benefit resident, commuter, disabled, and adult students.

The programming board and the student affairs department approved funding for the salsa band from the pot of money generated by the student activities fee. However, this meant that the dance had to be open to all Penn State students and we could not charge for admission to raise funds for the club. With the band paid for, the LSAB's job was to get the word out to the campus community by promoting and advertising the event. The student affairs department supplied decorations, and club members were responsible for putting them up on the day of the dance. And since the space being used for the event — the campus cafeteria — could only hold 200 people, club members offered free tickets to get a rough head count for the event. Students could bring friends, but everyone had to show a ticket at the door. Tickets proved they were a Penn State student or with a Penn State student. This admittedly is not a foolproof system, but it met our needs.

To advertise, the club used their color printer to make huge posters and flyers to be displayed and distributed around campus. Posters were hung in the student center and the library, and flyers were distributed all over campus. Messages were also posted on the campus's student listserv, but word-of-mouth really helped. In addition, two weeks before the dance was scheduled to be held, the club created a marvelous display of books and posters on salsa dancing and Latin American culture. Flyers about the dance were placed near the book display to help encourage more students, faculty, and staff to come.

On the evening of the dance over thirty students showed up for lessons during the hour before the dance and over sixty turned out for the dance. A member of the band continued to give lessons throughout the dance because the students were enjoying it so much. The band's attire was fabulous and they used a fascinating variety of instruments to produce the distinctive salsa sound and intricate rhythms. Though we had a good turnout, it was not quite as many as we had hoped. But it was enough to encourage us to do something like it again sometime. Our dance was a success. Not only did the students attend this fantastic affair, but we also had staff, faculty, and their families join the fun.

Tug-a-Bug for United Way

One day the library club received a call from our campus student affairs department asking if our Library Student Advisory Board would be interested in becoming a part of the 2007 Schuylkill United Way fund-raiser. We explained to the students that the Schuylkill United Way raises money to support sixteen local family service agencies and that all the money raised in Schuylkill County stays in Schuylkill County.[1] The United Way was having a "Tug-a-Bug" competition, which involved six teams in groups of eight, each pulling a Volkswagen Beetle for fifty yards down our campus's central mall walkway. The team who had the fastest time would win $5,000 donated to the Schuylkill United Way in their name. This would be a high-profile local event documented by the local print and radio news media. And the student affairs department had invited the Library Student Advisory Board to participate because they were community-centered, responsible, and would get the job done. This, of course, was met with much excitement from the club. This competition seemed like a good way to get involved with the community, while raising awareness about the club and our library.

Another element of the competition was a "most creative costumes" competition, with the winning team receiving $1,000 donated to the United Way in the team's name. Each team consisted of eight tuggers — four men and four women participants. To make everyone happy, and coincidentally tying in with our library's open house theme, our club decided to go with a pirate theme.

The day turned out to be phenomenal. The weather was perfect and the event attracted hundreds of onlookers. A local radio station even covered the event live and the local newspaper was on site to document it in print. I can't adequately describe how exciting it was to see our LSAB members compete in such a physical contest and for such a worthy cause. Not only were we contributing to a local charity, but also doing wonders to update the image of a library and a library club. I, Marianne, stood on the sidelines taking pictures of the event, feeling pride in what our club has become.

Taking turns in timed heats, each team swaggered up to the starting line. A local Volkswagen dealership supplied a 2008 Volkswagen Beetle to be tugged. After all the teams pulled the Beetle, the emcee announced that there was a tie. To my astonishment the contest had come down to our Library Student Advisory Board and the women's basketball team competing for the title.

They had to have a tiebreaker to determine the winner. You could feel the anticipation and excitement in the crowd and hear the mutterings of people guessing which team would win the tiebreaker. In the second heat the Library Student Advisory Board pulled the 2,700-pound Beetle fifty yards in 12.07 seconds, beating the women's basketball team's time of 12.31 seconds. We had won! The crowd was cheering. There were plenty of congratulations and hearty slaps on the back for a job well done. Members of the library club were interviewed by the newspaper and had their picture taken. Hannah Tracy, then president of the Library Student Advisory Board, was quoted in the Pottsville *Republican & Herald* saying, "We (the LSAB) try to do different things on campus, to help out the school and the community," she said. "Plus, it's fun."[2] Combining knowledge with experience, our team figured the best way to win was to not allow any slack in the rope. To accomplish this the team strategized to have our lead man, Jon Seiler, wrap the rope around his waist. His height and Naval Reserves training give him the ability to keep the rope taut while running — in combat boots! They also staggered the men and women of the team so that the strongest men were on each end. They really worked together to make a plan and get the job done.

The next day there was a lot of talk about the event and about how the library club had actually won. Kids on campus had a fun time chanting "The bookworms beat the jocks!" All the Tug-a-Bug participants received a gift bag containing goodies such as key chains, T-shirts, and food donated by event sponsors. And the United

Jonathan Seiler leads the LSAB to victory at the United Way Tug-a-Bug event.

Way invited the eight tuggers from the Library Student Advisory Board team to the closing breakfast of the United Way Campaign to thank them for their participation.

The winner of the best costume contest was not our Library Student Advisory Board, but a mixed faculty and staff team. The men wore Penn State cheerleaders' uniforms and the women wore the men's basketball team's uniforms. This was hilarious to see and everyone was glad when they won the $1,000 for United Way. Our team came in second in the costume contest with their pirate attire. This is just a small example of how you can take your club to a totally new level of activity and still represent your library in a positive manner.

Other Events

The Library Student Advisory Board has agreed to lend a hand to help other clubs on campus with a variety of events they have planned for the next year. These include the campus chapter of the NAACP, the United Minority Leaders, and the Environmental & Biology Club. The NAACP wants to work with our club to bring speakers in for Black History Month and Women's History Month. One of the speakers the groups are bringing in for Unity Day will talk with students on campus about hate crimes. The library will also help by creating displays on Martin Luther King, Jr., for Black History Month and recycling for Earth Day to raise awareness in the campus community about these events, while tying them into library collections.

March is the celebration and awareness month for Earth Day. This is a time to celebrate the progress that has been made in cleaning up our world by promoting land conservation, improving water and air quality, preserving our wildlife habitats, and other environmental conservation efforts. The library club was asked to assist the Environmental & Biology Club in their endeavor to get the entire campus community involved with Earth Day. Our club will help by creating a display on ways to help improve paper, newspaper, aluminum, and plastic recycling efforts on campus.

New Directions

As we look even further into the future of the Library Student Advisory Board at Penn State Schuylkill, we can envision many different directions in which the group could go. Perhaps you could use some of these ideas to get your own club started. However, since we encourage the students to lead the direction of the club, with some input from the library, what really lies ahead for us is unknown. Future leaders of the group are still scattered in high schools across the state, even the throughout the county. Who knows where they will take us?

Increased Advocacy Efforts

One path we would like to see the Library Student Advisory Board take is to increase their advocacy efforts. We want them to be confident in our abilities to provide the resources and services students need, to be well informed about what these resources and services are, and to be excited to share this with others. Whether in class, a meeting with a professor, chatting with friends, or out in the community promoting the club and campus, we hope they eventually will be able to engage people at a higher level about the library. To go beyond saying "we represent the library," to say "we represent the library and this is what the library can do for you." To show their peers or members of the local community that we have resources they might not even think to ask for, that our lending policies are favorable to students, that we do loan items to local community members. That the librarians and staff at the library are there to help them — and not just when they're desperate and have exhausted all their other options, but also to consult with at the *beginning* of a project.

This could be accomplished by the library staff sharing information with club members early each year, perhaps arming students with a small packet of information and some advanced research skills. A notion we might need to combat with some students is that we offer nothing significantly different from their high school or public library. In Pennsylvania, many K–12 schools offer the same online research databases as the public library through their membership in a statewide library consortium. In some places, the public library staff may be as familiar with students' assignments as the school library staff— something that doesn't happen once they get to college. We hope they would come to realize that not only do we have specialized research resources for college students at the undergraduate and graduate levels, but that we have experience with their assignments and perhaps even advanced training in the area of their research.

Others may have library anxiety, or "confusion, fear, and frustration felt by a library user, especially someone lacking experience, when faced with the need to find information in a library."[3] One way the club helps us defeat this fear is helping with the planning and execution of the library's open house event. We also believe that hearing about the library from a peer — how to navigate the library, who to see, what we have to offer — helps alleviate library anxiety. Again, this can be accomplished by arming club members with accurate information about the library. Thinking on a larger scale, perhaps one day some club students would be interested in attending a local ALA Advocacy Institute.[4]

Expanding Campus and Local Community Service

Our students seem to really enjoy doing community service, and as we discussed in chapter 1, many of them are coming to college with community service experience and from a culture that valued, or at least rewarded, community service. Looking beyond the library, our LSAB members enjoyed raising money for pediatric cancer and participating in "THON." Club members enjoyed participating in the Tug-a-Bug event for the United Way, benefiting local service organizations. Building on club members' interests in providing community service may help attract more students to the join the Library Student Advisory Board. Combining this interest with improved advocacy skills for promoting the library would be a particularly effective combination of interests.

We have already seen that as a direct result of the Library Student Advisory Board's campus and community service, we have experienced an increase in donations of used and new books, audio books, and DVDs to the library, as well as photographs to add to our local and campus history collections. Perhaps if we were able to combine library advocacy efforts with the students' interest in community service and work in coordination with the campus development office, the club and the library could recognize even larger donations. We need to keep in mind, of course, that the club advisor is simply a guiding voice from within the library and that all of this has to be something club members want to do and can get excited about doing to keep interest in the club high. Perhaps this is a project on which the Library Student Advisory Board could enter into a partnership with the library.

Developing Interest Groups

Since our Library Student Advisory Board has become quite large, it might be desirable for the club to splinter into interest groups. This way, members could focus on the aspect of the club they are most interested in, whether it be advocacy for the library, fund-raising, community service, or special events.

Return to the Library

After venturing into service projects on campus and in the local community, if there is indeed a cyclical nature to things, we wonder if eventually the club will return to their library roots, bringing lots of creative new ideas with them. As originally stated in the club's constitution, the purpose of the Library Student Advisory Board at Penn State Schuylkill is to "promote student input and involvement in library services and programming." Possible realms the club might expand upon include developing the book club and helping the library explore how and when they offer library services such as study space, help with technology (software and hardware) questions and problems, and research assistance.

The library book club was a suggestion of the Library Student Advisory Board and quickly became a student-staff collaboration. A member of the library staff helps the students select potential titles for the club, students interested in the book club vote on which title they would like to read next, and the library staff helps students secure library copies of the novel. We currently have about six to ten campus students, staff, and faculty interested in the book club, as well as a few people from the local community that participate as much as their schedules permit.

This is certainly a respectable size for a book club. Actually, it might be the ideal size to have a good discussion during the hour the book club meets. However, possible ways the LSAB could expand the book club include offering a more diverse array of title selections and tying in the book club with required reading for campus courses to encourage participation by more students. While it has typically selected best-seller novels for club reading, the club could also pursue a "contemporary classics" theme, or explore popular nonfiction such as biographies, travel writing, or food writing. There is certainly a market for best-selling novels and this does tie in nicely with the Library Student Advisory Board's donations to the library. However, we do encounter a number of students who are inspired by their college studies and wish to further explore the twentieth-century classics they were introduced to in high school (Steinbeck, Hemingway, Angelou, etc.). Food and travel writing tend to be easy reads and are common interests of large segments of the population. Biographies can be easy reads if they are well-written, but selecting a popular, well-known figure is probably the key to attracting students. Biographies of actors, musicians, or artists could be tied in with a movie night, musical performance, or art exhibition. Another realm to explore is books made into films, and the increasingly common phenomenon of films made into novels.

The club might also advise administrators on the variety of services and collections offered by the library. Trends in libraries such as a shift from reference desks to information commons, or the redesign of public work space to accommodate more group work and the technological gadgets students have in tow, involve realms where it would be more likely that the library would approach the club for advice, rather than the club suggesting these things to the library.

While our library has experienced an explosion in usage during its regular operating hours since the inception of the Library Student Advisory Board, we still occasionally receive the suggestion to extend the library's hours into the wee hours of the morning. In a small library such as ours, staffing so many hours in one day is problematic. For other libraries, the number of staff needed throughout the library to ensure the security of collections and equipment might be an issue. But if students seriously want an extended-hours study area, perhaps the Library Student Advisory Board could work together with library and campus administration to find a solution that works for everyone.

If your library is considering the development of an information commons — perhaps merging the research and technology help desks — a library student advisory board could be very helpful at making this marriage a success. Both parties are familiar with the types of questions they usually get from students, but there very well might be gray areas — questions and problems students haven't previously raised with anyone. These might entail problems with home technologies, advice on selecting a new computer, or perhaps the need to have a writing tutor stationed at the information commons. Student input on the planning of an information commons could be very helpful to the process.

For several years there have been discussions about the declining use of library reference services, leading to questions about the viability of this traditional form of assistance. Some librarians will tell you that while the number of questions they answer may have gone down, the quality or the difficulty of the questions have gone up. Others will tell you that many of their questions involve the public printer being out of paper. We think that it is up to each institution to answer the question of what to do about reference for themselves, but one way to go about it could be getting your library student advisory board involved in revamping reference or "research assistance." The club could help the library discover and explore alternative means for providing reference service, including various ways to use the power of the Internet, cell phones, or the notion of replacing the reference desk with in-office research assistance appointments. The library could also work with the club to explore the topics students are researching and how they go about tackling a research assignment, including what students typically look for in a good source. This could help with collection development, as well as both instruction and reference services.

Are You Ready?

It may seem that on our campus the Library Student Advisory Board has become a sort of "one-stop shop" for club participation. Our club does a little bit of everything—it plans social events and participates in local community service projects, while providing us advice when needed and raising money to purchase books, DVDs, video games, and video-game players for donation to the library. It may be true that we are a "one-stop shop," but that works for us. And it provides club members quite a bit of variety on our small campus. We hope that you can use our experience to build a club customized to your own needs. But remember that this is a student club—a group with its own agenda and interests—and it is providing a service to you. With mutual respect, the relationship between the library and a library student advisory board can be a wonderful marriage.

Epilogue, or, So, What Is Stopping You?

What is stopping you? You have read about *why* to start a student advisory board at your library, *how* to get a group started, how *our* Library Student Advisory Board has benefited our library, and what *your* club might be able to do through advising, advocacy, and fund-raising to help make your library more student-centered. We have tried to help you decide who in your library would best serve as the club advisor and who you might recruit as student members to get your club started, as well as how you might recruit more members over time. We have talked about all the people who can help you along the way, including colleagues at the library and staff in student affairs and other departments who will gladly help you make this idea a reality on your campus. *Where?* Well, the answer to that may be obvious. *When,* then, may be the question that is stopping you.

When will I be able to find the time to fit this into my busy schedule? When will I be able to find the time for proposals and training and recruiting and more meetings and fund-raisers and listening to clingy students?

And maybe these questions lead to others. Where am I going to find students interested in doing this? And who are we going to find to be the advisor? Would I be a good club advisor? Perhaps bringing you back to the question about time.

When Will I Find the Time?

You probably would not be reading this unless you really wanted to make your library a better place. You probably would not be reading this if you weren't looking for a new way to attract students to your library. Just remember that you are not alone.

Students are an essential part of the plan and should be doing much of the work themselves, especially if your library student advisory board is a regular club on campus. Much of the library's investment of time should be simply in finding a handful of students to get the club started and helping them through the process. And to do this, you will have the support of your student affairs department (or whichever department manages student organizations on your campus). The *required* duties of a club advisor are likely to be minimal: attend club meetings, discuss club goals and directions (be that guiding voice from within the library), and possibly serve as the budget supervisor. Marianne (our club advisor) has chosen to be more active — a role supported by our library administration. And we think the work she puts into the club and the encouragement and support she provides the students is a large part of what has made Penn State Schuylkill's club so successful.

So, just like with anything else, finding the time is just a matter of priorities. When considering your priorities, consider this:

- Are students important to your library?
- Would you like to improve your library's student-centeredness?
- Would you like to increase awareness among students about your library's collections and services?
- Would you like more student input on programming, or even collection development ideas?

If you answered yes to any of these questions, we think a library student advisory board can help you. A library student advisory board can take you in any or all of these directions. It can be whatever you need it to be; yours certainly does not have to be exactly like ours. Investing some time and effort into your library student advisory board and making it one of your priorities will pay off. We believe that with a little bit of effort you will find increased usage of your library facilities, collections and services.

Where Will I Find the Students?

Marianne has her own story about how she recruited her first members to the group, but not everyone might be so lucky to have a college-bound son with lots of friends to talk into starting a library club, though some of you may be in a similar situation, or know someone with a college-age child to help recruit new members. Others may have even greater opportunities to attract a diverse and interested group of students in order to get your club started. Think about those students you see in the library all the time. Whether they think the library is too loud, too quiet, or needs an espresso machine and an attractive barista — they probably have ideas for ways the library could be more student-centered and likely have some interest in doing so. We have observed over the years that the majority of our student workers sought a job at the library because they love libraries or at least have warm memories of the library from childhood. Although the rest seem to want to work in the library because they think it is a good place to do their homework while they are working, it is likely that you will be able to entice at least a couple of student workers into starting a club.

And if you still need more students to get the club started, start talking with friends and colleagues about what it is that you want to do. They might know students who would make good candidates for the inaugural group of club members and be in a position to help you recruit them to the club. Or, at the very least, they can help you by spreading the word about your club to others. Maybe they have a college-age student at home, or a neighbor who does. Maybe they have a student in their class who has, unbeknownst to you, written an "ode to my library" for class and would make an outstanding club member.

Try contacting faculty who are library supporters and regularly have you visit their classrooms or have their students use the library. Ask them if they can suggest any students who might be willing to join your club. With today's library models combining the brick-and-mortar building with electronic collections and services, it is entirely possible to have regular and efficient library users who never or rarely step foot in the physical building or seek face-to-face assistance from the staff. If you can capture these students and entice them to join your library student advisory board, there is the potential to learn valuable information about your electronic resources. You might learn what it would take to get these virtual users into the library, or even learn more about their typical usage of electronic library resources — information that can be difficult to glean accurately from database usage reports.

Still need more recruitment ideas? Talk with the advisors of other clubs and organizations on campus to see how they got started, or how they recruit new members. Or pay a visit to the staff in your student affairs department. There are always a few students who seem to be involved in everything and might be interested in getting involved with your club too. These students can give insight into what other groups are doing and have experience with the way other clubs are run, so they can make good officers for your club. These students might also have ideas for fund-raisers and programs based on past experience.

Also look beyond the obvious — the students you regularly see using the library and your library's work-study student population. Consider looking to campus students you know in a social context beyond your job — perhaps through a religious or volunteer organization. If you regularly attend or participate in campus sporting events, try recruiting members of the team or talking about the club with the coach to see if they have students to recommend. Even if the players are not able to recognize you as a regular enthusiastic team supporter, you will have a starting point for your conversation — a mutual interest in the sport and pride in your college or university. The same goes for students involved in music, theater, and other artistic pursuits, or special-interest and service organizations such as the fraternities and sororities on your campus. At other Penn State campuses, these students often make use of the library, and meeting the needs of their large study groups can be challenging. There may well be individuals in these groups with an interest in helping the library help their group meet their study and research needs. When you approach these students, you will not only be able to relate the club to general interests of all students, but to the specific interest of those students.

The above suggestions are hypothetical, not tried-and-true methods for recruiting students, but we hope that they make the notion of starting a library student advisory board seem like a real possibility for your library. We were able to get great ideas and honest feedback from our admittedly most unlikely users — the people we wanted to attract back into the library. We say "back into the library" because, though it may have been a long time, you will often find that at one point — maybe when they were very, very young — these kids used to enjoy reading and going to the library with their parents for story time, summer reading programs, or just to borrow books.

Regardless of your method, when recruiting students or even talking about the idea for a club with friends and colleagues, be sure that your enthusiasm and excitement for the club is palpable. These emotions are contagious and the feeling conveyed will do as much to recruit students to the group as simply asking them to join.

Would I Be a Good Club Advisor?

Assuming the potential club advisor will be doing at least some of the recruiting for your library student advisory board's initial member recruitment, a good club advisor would be someone who can convey a sense of excitement and enthusiasm about the club. Other traits of a good club advisor might include being a good listener, having a good attention for detail, being energetic, and having a good rapport with the younger generation.

Are you more of a stoic than someone who easily lets their emotion bubble to the surface? There is still hope. Those other characteristics — such as a natural rapport with students or attention to detail and good organization skills — will also help you recruit students to the club.

Does My Library Really Need This?

A library student advisory board such as the one found at Penn State Schuylkill will help you build a good working relationship with the student body on your campus by giving students a voice in the library. Club members can provide a student voice on library services, collections, or even offer advice on the general library atmosphere to help you meet students' needs and improve your library's student-centeredness.

Epilogue

Some student needs, such as a basic need for information, will always remain the same. However, other student needs change with each generation. Each year students come in with a slightly different set of research skills and skill gaps. There are gains in some areas of technology literacy and widening gaps in others. The amount of information available to students increases dramatically every day. The way we harness and organize this information is changing too. How do we connect students to the best information? And how do we most effectively provide services to our students? Each generation of students seems to embrace a different communication technology: e-mail, IM, texting, personal social network profiles. Which ones do we choose to embrace to provide better service? Which ones do we take a pass on?

If you think a library student advisory board would be successful at improving and promoting your library, it is time to get one started. If not, take another look at studies of today's students, such *Studying Students: The Undergraduate Research Project at the University of Rochester.*[1] While study results cannot be universally applied, it is likely that something in the report will resonate with you. And if any of these findings do remind you of your library, perhaps it is time to take some action. If you are ready to improve the student-centeredness of your library, consider starting a library student advisory board to help you find out what students need and to have students advocate for the library on your behalf.

The students you need are out there!

Appendix A

Club Calendar at a Glance

Throughout the Year

- Keep in regular contact with club members. Remind students about meetings, fund-raiser goals, deadlines, and special projects, and publicly welcome new members, but avoid overuse of reminders — students will stop reading your messages altogether. Consider methods most suitable for your membership:

    ◄ E-mail

    ◄ Course management system (for example, WebCT, Blackboard) group space

    ◄ Public social network (for example, Facebook, MySpace) group space

- Collect important documents for club files and annual report, including financial records, receipts, contracts, and meeting minutes.

- Collect photos, programs, and other items for "victory log" (end-of-year scrapbook).

- Have students prepare articles about their activities for club, library, and campus newsletters.

- Encourage library staff to attend meetings and to seek student input (and club assistance when possible) on library event planning and any decisions that will have an impact on usability or the library as a student space.

- Update club Web site as necessary. You may wish to appoint a member as webmaster, make this a regular duty of an existing officer, or make webmaster duties a leadership position in your constitution.

Before Start of Fall Semester

- Plan to apply for regular university funding. Consider what funds will be used for and how much you need to request.

- Check and finalize details (room and equipment requests, dates on student affairs calendar and other university calendars) for regular annual events and fund-raisers (for example, car wash).

- E-mail club members to remind them of the first meeting and other important fall dates — an early welcome back to campus. Give them a reason to be excited about coming back to campus.

- Update or revise club recruitment info (posters, flyers, bookmarks) for fall recruitment opportunities (for example, library open house and activities fair). Print and have items ready to go at a moment's notice.

- Check on club's financial account; ensure club's records match reality and try to resolve any issues before the start of the semester. Have an accurate balance for your new treasurer in the fall.

First Week Students Are Back On Campus

- Welcome club members back to campus and encourage them to stop by for a visit. Find out about their summer and ask what ideas they might have for the club this year.

- Set up a brief meeting with your club leaders and finalize plans for first meeting.

- Ask leaders to help prepare folders for new and returning members. Include a copy of the club's constitution, calendar of important events, library's hours, and important phone numbers (possibly in form of a bookmark), and any other important items.
- Remind members of any fall club recruitment opportunities (for example, activities fair and library open house). Find a few who can commit to helping out at the events.

August–September

- Submit application for university funds earmarked for club use. (Typically through student affairs department or student government.)
- A few days before club recruitment events, remind members who've agreed to help of date, time, and location of event. Consider whether extra time is needed for setup and teardown.
- At recruitment events, provide literature about the club and examples of its accomplishments. Share some plans for the upcoming year. Show how students can make a difference. Have a colorful display (using balloons, for example) and freebies if possible. Collect names and contact information of any students interested in the club. Following the event, contact prospective members with additional information. Remind them of the next club meeting.
- Encourage club member participation in the library open house or other orientation activities. Put a student face on the library; provide an informed peer to impart essential information and answer questions such as, "Why do I need to know this?" and "Will I really need to use the library?"
  - ◁ Provide club members with important information about the library

before the event. Avoid spread of misinformation.
  - ◁ Following event, get member input (on what worked well and what didn't) to inform planning for next year.
- At first meeting, discuss and vote on a fall fund-raiser and start organizing.

October

- Inform all club members about fall fund-raiser and start selling.

November

- Fund-raiser wrap-up; collect and deposit money. Prepare suggestion box or online survey to collect student requests for popular books, DVDs, games.
- Begin planning special events for spring semester; fill out necessary forms (for example, room and equipment requests) and record date on appropriate activity calendars.

December

- Show appreciation and say goodbye to any club members graduating or leaving at the end of this semester.
- Hold elections for midyear replacement officers (if you have any officers leaving).
- Brainstorm ideas for spring fund-raiser.
- Offer end-of-semester stress relievers (for example, food and games) if possible.

January

- Regroup after holiday break; get motivated for spring semester.
- Discuss plans for spring and remind students of planned events and ongoing projects.
- Finish discussion and vote on spring fund-raiser. Begin organizing.

February

- Get members thinking about elections; let students know which officer positions will be open and remind them of duties of each position.
- Start selling, if holding another fundraiser.

March

- Apply for any remaining university funds, if available.
- Motivate after spring break to push through to the end of the year.
- Remind students of upcoming elections and job responsibilities.
- Wrap up fund-raiser.

April

- Hold elections; have new officers elected for fall start working with current officers to pass on knowledge and any important documents.
- Fund-raiser wrap-up; collect and deposit money. Prepare suggestion box or online survey to collect student requests for popular books, DVDs, games.
- Begin discussing special events for next year; select dates if possible and start completing necessary paperwork (room and equipment request forms, etc.).
- Start work on "victory log."

May

- Hold new-officers meeting to start planning for next year; have new officers start working with old officers to pass on information.
- Show appreciation and say goodbye to any club members graduating or leaving at the end of this semester.
- Brainstorm ideas for fall fund-raiser.

- Offer end-of-semester stress relievers (for example, food and games) if possible.

Summer (May–August)

- Prepare annual reports of club accomplishments for student affairs and/or library administration.
- Meet with student affairs to go over campus calendar and get your events listed; avoid conflicts if possible.
- Finish completing necessary forms (room and equipment requests) for special events on the club's fall calendar.
- Make sure club funds are in order.
- Periodically contact club members; tell them about what you have been working on over the summer and ask what they have been doing.
- Investigate possible grants.
- Investigate possible fund-raisers and compile info to share with students at the first meeting in the fall.

Club Calendar Year at a Glance

January

- regroup after holiday break; get motivated for spring semester
- discuss plans for spring and remind students about important dates
- discuss spring fund-raiser
- discuss any new or proposed changes to the library with students

February

- get members thinking about elections; remind them of each position's duties

Appendix A

March

- apply for any remaining university funds
- motivate after spring break to push through to the end of the year
- remind students about April elections

April

- hold elections
- have new officers elected for fall start work with current officers
- begin discussing special events and projects for next year
- work on "victory log"

May

- meet with new officers to start planning for next year
- show appreciation and say goodbye to any club members not returning next year
- brainstorm ideas for fall fund-raiser

June

- prepare annual report
- get club events on the campus calendar
- complete any paperwork needed for special events
- make sure club funds are in order

July

- stay in contact with club members
- investigate possible grants and apply
- investigate potential fund-raisers
- verify event details
- revise and stock up on recruitment info

August

- plan to apply for funding
- e-mail club members about important dates; ask to stop by once back to campus
- check club fund balance
- prepare folders with important club info

September

- meet with club leaders
- apply for funds
- recruit new members
- participate in library orientation activities; talk with students about library
- decide on a fund-raiser and get started

October

- big fund-raiser push

November

- fund-raiser wrap-up; collect student input on purchases
- begin to plan special events for spring semester
- get club events on the campus calendar

December

- show appreciation and say goodbye to any club members leaving after this semester
- elect midyear replacement officers
- discuss spring fund-raiser

Appendix B

Sample Bookmarks

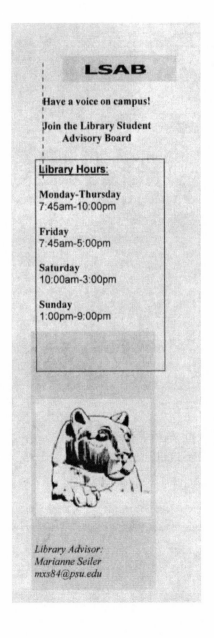

Appendix B

LSAB

MAKE A DIFFER-

Join the Library Student Advisory Board

Library Hours:

Monday-Thursday
7:45am-10:00pm
Friday
7:45am-5:00pm
Saturday
10:00am-3:00pm
Sunday
1:00pm-9:00pm

LSAB

Library Hours:

Monday-Thursday
7:45am-10:00pm
Friday
7:45am-5:00pm
Saturday
10:00am-3:00pm
Sunday
1:00pm-9:00pm

Join the Library Student Advisory Board

Visit on the Web!

www.libraries.psu.edu/schuylkill

Appendix C

LSAB Library User Satisfaction Survey

1. How many times a week do you use the library?

Every day
Once or twice a week
Occasionally
Never

2. Did your professors ever refer you to the library?

Every day
Once or twice a week
Occasionally
Never

3. Do you use the reference collection?

Every day
Once or twice a week
Occasionally
Never

4. Are you satisfied with the selection of DVDs?

Very satisfied
Satisfied
Neutral
Dissatisfied
Very dissatisfied

5. Do you read the leisure magazines in the library? (*Rolling Stone, Prevention, Sports Illustrated*, etc.)

Every day
Once or twice a week
Occasionally
Never

6. Do you know how to use The CAT (online catalog)?

Yes
A little
Not really
No

7. Do you know the library has laptops you can sign out?

Yes
No

8. Have you ever signed out one of the library's laptops?

Yes
No

9. Do you ever use your personal laptop in the library?

Yes
No

10. Do you use the study rooms in the library?

Every day
Once or twice a week
Occasionally
Never

11. Do you ever use the white boards in the study rooms?

Every day
Once or twice a week
Occasionally
Never

12. Do you use the VCR or DVD players?

Every day
Once or twice a week
Occasionally
Never

13. Have you ever asked for help?

Yes
No

14. If you are unable to find something, is it easy to get help?

Yes
No

15. If you need help with your research is it available to you?

Always
Sometimes
Never

16. Do you know the library has a copy machine for your use?

Yes
No

Comments:

17. What do you like to read: (circle as many as apply)

Biographies
Suspense/mysteries/thrillers
Science fiction/fantasy
Graphic novels
Short stories/essays
ChickLit
GuyLit
Historical fiction
Other fiction
Other nonfiction
I don't like to read

18. Do you use audio books?

Yes
No

19. Do you ever have problems finding an available computer?

Always
Sometimes
Never

20. Rate your overall experience with the library? (5 being the best)

5   4   3   2   1

Sample Wii Authorization Form

Ciletti Memorial Library—Authorization for Wii Loan

A Wii game console is available at the Circulation Desk for loan to registered Penn State students, faculty, and staff. This unit is available on a first-come, first-served basis and cannot be reserved ahead of time.

By your signature below, you, as the borrower of the Wii, agree to use this unit in accordance with all Penn State University guidelines. Specifically,

- Use of the Wii is only within Ciletti Memorial Library. It is not permitted to leave the premises for any reason.
- The Wii must be returned directly to a staff member at the circulation desk no later than 15 minutes before the library closes on the same day on which unit was borrowed. Do not simply leave the unit at the circulation desk unattended. Ring bell for service.
- If the Wii is not returned to the Circulation Desk within two (2) hours, it will be subject to overdue fees of $1.00/hour for each hour overdue. If the Wii is not returned prior to closing on the same day, it will be presumed lost and replacement fees, in addition to overdue fees, may be assessed.
- The borrower of the Wii assumes full responsibility for damage, loss, or theft. If damage occurs to the unit or any of its components or accessories, charges for repair or replacement will be imposed.
- Student borrowers authorize Penn State to charge their Student Accounts for repair and replacement fees if necessary. Penn State employee borrowers authorize the Libraries, after appropriate notice, to deduct from their paycheck any fees incurred.
- When borrowing the Wii, all components must remain in the case. All components are charged separately to the borrower.
- Do not leave the unit unattended for any reason!

Borrower's signature _____ Date: _____
Phone number _____ Access Account ID: _____
Borrower's PSU ID number _____
CHECKOUT Inspection Checklist:
Date/Time: _____ Staff initials: _____ Patron initials: _____
Console _____ Remote 1 _____ Remote 2 _____
CHECKIN Inspection Checklist:
Nunchuk 1 _____ Nunchuk 2 _____ Sensor Bar _____ Console Stand _____
AC Adapter _____ AV Cable _____

Chapter Notes

Chapter 1

1. Association of Research Libraries, *ARL Statistics*, Interactive Edition, University of Virginia Library, http://fisher.lib.virginia.edu/arl/index.html (accessed April 24, 2007).

2. Pennsylvania State University, "Welcome to Penn State," http://www.psu.edu/admissions/whypsu/glance (accessed June 2, 2008).

3. William J. Buck, "The Schuylkill," in *Bean's History of Montgomery County, Pennsylvania*, edited by Theodore W. Bean (Philadelphia: Everts & Peck, 1884), http://ftp.rootsweb.com/pub/usgenweb/pa/montgomery/history/local/mchb0010.txt (accessed June 2, 2008).

4. Robert Grimm, Jr., et al. *Building Active Citizens: The Role of Social Institutions on Teen Volunteering*, Youth Helping America series (Washington, DC: Corporation for National and Community Service, November 2005), 2, http://www.nationalservice.gov/pdf/05_1130_LSA_YHA_study.pdf (accessed June 2, 2008).

5. U.S. Dept. of Labor, Bureau of Labor Statistics, "Volunteering in the United States, 2006," (Jan. 10, 2007), USDL 07–0019, http://www.impactgiveback.org/PDF/VolunteeringUnitedStates2006.pdf (accessed June 2, 2008).

6. Kimberly Spring, Nathan Dietz, and Robert Grimm, Jr., *Educating for Active Citizenship: Service-Learning, School-Based Service and Youth Civic Engagement*, Youth Helping America series, Brief 2 (Washington, DC: Corporation for National and Community Service, March 2006), 3, http://www.nationalservice.gov/pdf/06_0323_SL_briefing.pdf (accessed June 2, 2008).

7. Ibid., 5.

8. "Service-Learning is...," National Service-Learning Clearinghouse, n.d., http://www.servicelearning.org/welcome_to_service-learning/service-learning_is/index.php (accessed June 2, 2008).

9. Spring, Dietz, and Grimm, Jr., 1.

10. Ibid., 9.

11. "Standards of Quality for School-Based and Community-Based Service Learning," Alliance for Service-Learning in Education Reform, March 1995, http://www.servicelearning.org/filemanager/download/12/asler95.pdf (accessed June 2, 2008).

12. Corporation for National Community Service, http://www.nationalservice.org (accessed April 24, 2007).

13. Spring, Dietz, and Grimm, Jr., 1.

14. Ibid.

15. Robert Grimm, Jr., et al. *Building Active Citizens*, 11.

16. Spring, Dietz, and Grimm, Jr., 27.

17. Robert Grimm, Jr., et al. *Building Active Citizens*, 2.

18. Ibid., 9.

19. Ibid., 2.

20. Spring, Dietz, and Grimm, Jr., 5.

21. Robert Grimm, Jr., et al. *Building Active Citizens*, 11.

22. Peter C. Scales and Eugene C. Roehlkepartain, *Community Service and Service-Learning in U.S. Public Schools, 2004: Findings from a National Survey* (St. Paul, MN: National Youth Leadership Council, 2004), 8, http://www.search-institute.org/whatsnew/2004G2GCompleteSurvey.pdf (accessed June 2, 2008).

23. Robert Grimm, Jr., et al. *Building Active Citizens*, 11.

24. Mark Hugo Lopez and Brent A. Elrod, *College Attendance and Civic Engagement Among 18 to 25 Year Olds, Fact Sheet*, ED494035 (College Park, MD: Center for Information and Research on Civic Learning & Engagement, School of Public Policy, University of Maryland, 2006).

25. Scott Keeter, Cliff Zukin, Molly Andolina, and Krista Jenkins, *The Civic and Political Health of the Nation: A Generational Portrait* (College Park, MD: Center for Information on Research on Civic Learning and Engagement, School of Public Policy, University of Maryland, 2002), http://www.civicyouth.org/research/products/Civic_Political_Health.pdf (accessed June 2, 2008).

26. Robert Grimm, Jr., et al. *Building Active Citizens*, 11, 13.

27. Spring, Dietz, and Grimm, Jr., 28; for more about the relationship between school-based service and positive youth development, see Shelley H. Billig, "Research on K–12 School-Based Service-Learning," *Phi Delta Kappan* 81, no. 9 (May 2000): 658–664; Judith Torney-Purta, "The School's Role in Developing Civic Engagement: A Study of Adolescents in Twenty-Eight Countries," *Applied Developmental Science* 6, no. 4 (2002): 203–212; Miranda Yates and James Youniss, "A Developmental Perspective on Community Service in Adolescence," *Social Development* 5, no. 1 (March 1996): 85–111.

28. Tracy L. Skipper and Roxanne Argo, *Involvement in Campus Activities and the Retention of First-Year College Students* (Columbia, SC: University of South Carolina, National Resource Center for The First-Year Experience and Students in Transition, 2003), ix–x.

29. Ibid., x.

30. Ibid., ix–xx.

31. Charles C. Schroeder, "Meeting the Changing Needs of Students," in *Involvement in Campus Activities and the Retention of First-Year College Students,* edited by Tracy L. Skipper and Roxanne Argo (Columbia, SC: University of South Carolina, National Resource Center for The First-Year Experience and Students in Transition, 2003), 24.

32. Ibid., 20; to learn more about characteristics of today's students, see any of the books about "millennials" or the "Net Generation," such as: Neil Howe and William Strauss, *Millennials Go to College: Strategies for a New Generation on Campus: Recruiting and Admissions, Campus Life, and the Classroom* (Washington, DC: American Association of Collegiate Registrars and Admissions Officers, 2003); Neil Howe and William Strauss, *Millennials Rising:*

The Next Great Generation (New York: Vintage Books, 2000).

33. Schroeder, 26.

34. M. H. Bedford and P. E. Durkee, "Retention: Some More Ideas," *NASPA Journal* 27, no. 2 (winter 1989): 168–171, quoted in Jonathan C. Dooley and Kathy M. Shellogg, "Developing Curricular and Co-Curricular Leadership Programs," in *Involvement in Campus Activities and the Retention of First-Year College Students,* edited by Tracy L. Skipper and Roxanne Argo (Columbia, SC: University of South Carolina, National Resource Center for The First-Year Experience and Students in Transition, 2003), 77.

Chapter 3

1. Norbert W. Dunkel and John H. Schuh, *Advising Student Groups and Organizations* (San Francisco: Jossey-Bass, 1998), 3.

2. Ibid., 73.

3. Dale Carnegie, *How to Win Friends & Influence People* (New York: Simon and Schuster, 1982).

4. Ed Bernacki, "Exactly What is 'Thinking Outside the Box'?" *CanadaOne Magazine,* April 2002, http://www.canadaone.com/ezine/april02/out_of_the_box_thinking.html (accessed June 3, 2008).

Chapter 4

1. "The Librarian Action Figure," Archie McPhee, http://www.mcphee.com/laf (accessed June 4, 2008).

2. See Kara Jesella, "A Hipper Crowd of Shushers," *New York Times,* July 8, 2007.

3. Patrick is referring to support from upper levels of administration in the Capital College and Capital College Libraries (still a part of the University Libraries). At that time, the Schuylkill and Harrisburg campuses were sister campuses comprising the Capital College, with college administration located at the Harrisburg campus. Later, university reorganization would separate the Schuylkill Campus from Capital College and move it to the University College, where administration is centralized at the University Park Campus.

Chapter 6

1. James Swan, *Fundraising for Libraries* (New York: Neal-Schuman Publishers, 2002), 102.

Chapter 7

1. Visit the American Library Association Store at http://www.alastore.ala.org (accessed June 4, 2008).

2. If you use Microsoft Publisher, the company has great instructions for setting up a custom publication to create bookmarks, "Can I create a bookmark in Publisher?" http://office.microsoft.com/en-us/publisher/HA0123364 81033.aspx (accessed June 4, 2008).

3. The mission of the Information Systems Committee is to review and make recommendations relating to information systems (academic computing and academic software, library functions, and instructional services) facilities and services, including long-range planning and development.

Chapter 8

1. See also Rebecca Merritt Bichel and Ellysa Stern Cahoy, "A Luau in the Library? A New Model of Library Orientation," *College and Undergraduate Libraries* 11, no. 1 (2004): 49–60; Ann Goebel Brown, Betty Dance, Judith R. J. Johnson and Sandra Weingart, "Librarians Don't Bite: Assessing Library Orientation for Freshmen," *Reference Services Review* 32, no. 4 (2004): 394–403; and Anthony J. Onwuegbuzie, Qun G. Jiao, and Sharon L. Bostick, *Library Anxiety: Theory, Research, and Applications.* (Lanham, MD: Scarecrow Press, 2004).

Chapter 9

1. Lynn Sutton and H. David Womack, "Got Game? Hosting Game Night in an Academic Library," *College & Research Libraries News* 67, no 3 (March 2006): 173–176.

Chapter 10

1. "About Us," Schuylkill United Way, http://www.schuylkillunitedway.org/about.htm (accessed June 8, 2008).

2. Kristen M. Scatton, "Volunteers Pull Bug for United Way," *Republican & Herald* (Pottsville, Pennsylvania), November 2, 2007.

3. Joan M. Reitz, "Library Anxiety," *Online Dictionary for Library and Information Science*, http://lu.com/odlis_l.cfm (accessed June 4, 2008).

4. "Issues and Advocacy," American Library Association, http://www.ala.org/ala/issues/issuesadvocacy.cfm (accessed June 4, 2008).

Epilogue

1. For an overview of this study, see Ann Marshall, Vickie Burns and Judi Briden, "Know Your Students: Rochester's Two-Year Ethnographic Study Reveals What Students Do on Campus and How the Library Fits In," *Library Journal* 132, no. 18 (November 1, 2007): 26–29. For the complete study results, see Nancy Fried Foster and Susan Gibbons, eds., *Studying Students: The Undergraduate Research Project at the University of Rochester* (Chicago: Association of College and Research Libraries, 2007).

Bibliography

Association of Research Libraries. *ARL Statistics*, Interactive Edition. University of Virginia Library, http://fisher.lib.virginia.edu/arl/index.html (accessed April 24, 2007).

Barber, Peggy, and Linda D. Crowe. *Getting Your Grant: A How-To-Do-It Manual For Librarians*. New York: Neal-Schuman, 1993.

Barksdale, Ken, and Charles C. Hay III. "Friendly Development: Organizing and Using a Friends Group in Academic Library Development." *Kentucky Libraries* 61 (1997): 16–23.

Bedford, Marilyn H., and Peter E. Durkee. "Retention: Some More Ideas." *NASPA Journal* 27, no. 2 (Winter 1989): 168–171.

Bell, Arthur H., and Dayle M. Smith. *Motivating Yourself for Achievement*. Upper Saddle River, NJ: Prentice Hall, 2003.

Benefiel, Candace R., Wendi Arant, and Elaine Gass. "A New Dialog: A Student Advisory Committee in an Academic Library." *Journal of Academic Librarianship* 25, no. 2 (March 1999): 111–113.

Bernacki, Ed. "Exactly What is 'Thinking Outside the Box'?" *CanadaOne Magazine*, April 2002, http://www.canadaone.com/ezine/april02/out_of_the_box_thinking.html (accessed June 3, 2008).

Bichel, Rebecca Merritt, and Ellysa Stern Cahoy. "A Luau in the Library? A New Model of Library Orientation." *College and Undergraduate Libraries* 11, no. 1 (2004): 49–60.

Billig, Shelley H. "Research on K-12 School-Based Service-Learning." *Phi Delta Kappan* 81, no. 9 (May 2000): 658–664.

Bolton, Judy. "Twenty-eight Years as Friends." *Mississippi Libraries* 55 (Spring 1981): 10–12.

Brown, Ann Goebel, Sandra Weingart, Judith R. J. Johnson, and Betty Dance. "Librarians Don't Bite: Assessing Library Orientation for Freshmen." *Reference Services Review* 32, no. 4 (2004): 394–403.

Bryans, Nancy R. "Library Volunteers Can Make a Difference." *Colorado Libraries* 25, no. 1 (Spring 1999): 42.

Buck, William J. "The Schuylkill." In *Bean's History of Montgomery County, Pennsylvania*, edited by Theodore W. Bean. Philadelphia: Everts & Peck, 1884. Online at http://ftp.rootsweb.com/pub/usgenweb/pa/montgomery/history/local/mchb0010.txt (accessed June 2, 2008).

Carnegie, Dale. *How to Win Friends & Influence People*. New York: Simon and Schuster, 1982.

Clark, Charlene K. "Getting Started with Annual Funds in Academic Libraries." *Journal of Library Administration* 12, no. 4 (1990): 73–87.

Collins, Rowland Lee. "Friendship and Greatness." *CLIC Quarterly* 3 (December 1984): 22–25.

Corson-Finnerty, Adam, and Laura Blanchard. "Using the Web to Find Old Friends and E-Friends." *American Libraries* 29, no. 4 (April 1998): 90–91.

Cress, Christine M., Helen S. Astin, Kathleen Zimmerman-Oster, and John C. Burkhardt. "Developmental Outcomes of College Student's Involvement in Leadership Activities." *Journal of College Student Development* 42, no. 1 (January/February 2001): 15–27.

Bibliography

Dolnick, Sandy. *Friends of Libraries Sourcebook*. Chicago: American Library Association, 1996.

Dooley, Jonathan C., and Kathy M. Shellogg. "Developing Curricular and Co-Curricular Leadership Programs." In *Involvement in Campus Activities and the Retention of First-Year College Students*, edited by Tracy L. Skipper and Roxanne Argo (Columbia, SC: University of South Carolina, National Resource Center for The First-Year Experience and Students in Transition, 2003), 75–85.

Dunkel, Norbert W., and John H. Schuh. *Advising Student Groups & Organizations*. San Francisco: Jossey-Bass, 1998.

Ferguson, Daniel. "Friends of the Library Groups: Implications for Promotion of Library Interests." *Australian Library Journal* 40 (November 1991): 328–335.

Foster, Nancy Fried, and Susan Gibbons, eds. *Studying Students: The Undergraduate Research Project at the University of Rochester*. Chicago: Association of College and Research Libraries, 2007.

Gerding, Stephanie K., and Pamela H. MacKellar. *Grants for Libraries: A How-To-Do-It Manual for Librarians*. New York: Neal-Schuman, 2006.

Grimm, Robert, Jr., et al. *Building Active Citizens: The Role of Social Institutions on Teen Volunteering*, Youth Helping America series. Washington, DC: Corporation for National and Community Service, November 2005. http://www.nationalservice.gov/pdf/05_1130_LSA_YHA_study.pdf (accessed June 2, 2008).

Haeuser, Michael. "Promoting Innovative Management and Services." *College & Research Libraries News* 49, no. 7 (July/August 1988): 419–422.

_____. "What Friends Are For: Gaining Financial Independence." *Wilson Library Bulletin* 60, no. 9 (May 1986): 25–27.

Herring, Mark Youngblood. *Raising Funds with Friends Groups*. New York: Neal-Schuman, 2004.

Hoadley, Irene B. "Future Perfect: The Library and Its Friends." *Library Administration & Management* 8, no. 3 (Summer 1994): 161–165.

Hopkins, James. "The Friends of the Air Force Academy Library: Friends in Deed!" *Colorado Libraries* 20 (Spring 1994): 37–39.

Howe, Neil, and William Stauss. *Millennials Go to College: Strategies for a New Generation on Campus: Recruiting and Admissions, Campus Life, and the Classroom*. Washington, DC: American Association of Collegiate Registrars and Admissions Officers, 2003.

_____. *Millennials Rising: The Next Great Generation*. New York: Vintage Books, 2000.

"Icebreakers, Warmups, Energizers, & Deinhibitizers." Wilderdom.com. http://wilderdom.com/games/Icebreakers.html (accessed June 4, 2008).

Jesella, Kara. "A Hipper Crowd of Shushers." *New York Times*, July 8, 2007.

Karsh, Ellen, and Arlen Sue Fox. *The Only Grant-Writing Book You'll Ever Need*. New York: Carroll & Graf, 2006.

Keeter, Scott, Cliff Zukin, Molly Andolina, and Krista Jenkins. *The Civic and Political Health of a Nation: A Generational Portrait*. College Park, MD: Center for Information on Research on Civic Learning and Engagement, School of Public Policy, University of Maryland, 2002. http://www.civicyouth.org/research/products/Civic_Political_Health.pdf (accessed June 2, 2008).

Komives, Susan R., Julie E. Owen, Susan D. Longerbeam, Felicia C. Mainella, and Laura Osteen. "Developing a Leadership Identity: A Grounded Theory." *Journal of College Student Development* 46, no. 6 (November/December 2005): 593–611.

Linscome, Mary L. "Friends of the Libraries Reach Out." *Colorado Libraries* 26, no. 3 (2000): 6–8.

Lopez, Mark Hugo, and Brent A. Elrod. *College Attendance and Civic Engagement Among 18 to*

Bibliography

25 Year Olds, Fact Sheet. ED494035. College Park, MD: Center for Information and Research on Civic Learning & Engagement, School of Public Policy, University of Maryland, 2006.

Magnan, Robert. *147 Practical Tips for Using Icebreakers with College Students.* Madison, WI: Atwood, 2005.

Marshall, Ann, Vickie Burns, and Judi Briden. "Know Your Students: Rochester's Two-Year Ethnographic Study Reveals What Students Do on Campus and How the Library Fits In." *Library Journal* 132, no. 18 (November 1, 2007): 26–29.

Morrison, James L., Jo Rha, and Audrey Helfman. "Learning Awareness, Student Engagement, and Change: A Transformation in Leadership Development." *Journal of Education for Business* 79, no. 1 (September/October 2003): 11–17.

Munch, Janet Butler. "College Library Friends Groups in New York, New Jersey, and Connecticut." *College & Research Libraries* 49, no. 5 (September 1988): 442–447.

Onwuegbuzie, Anthony J., Qun G. Jiao, and Sharon L. Bostick. *Library Anxiety: Theory, Research, and Applications.* Lanham, MD: Scarecrow Press, 2004.

Pennsylvania State University. "Welcome to Penn State." http://www.psu.edu/admissions/why psu/glance (accessed June 2, 2008).

Rea, Barbara S. "The Evolution of a Friends Group: Washington University Libraries' Bookmark Society." *Show-Me Libraries* 36 (September 1985): 19–23.

Reinders, Heinz, and James Youniss. "School-Based Required Community Service and Civic Development in Adolescents." *Applied Developmental Science* 10, no. 1 (January 2006): 2–12.

Reitz, Joan M. "Library Anxiety," *Online Dictionary for Library and Information Science,* http://lu.com/odlis_l.cfm (accessed June 4, 2008).

Sartori, Eve. "Friends of the Libraries, University of Nebraska-Lincoln." *Nebraska Library Association Quarterly* 23 (Summer 1992): 24–26.

Scales, Peter C., and Eugene C. Roehlkepartain. *Community Service and Service-Learning in U.S. Public Schools, 2004: Findings from a National Survey.* St. Paul, MN: National Youth Leadership Council, 2004. http://www.search-institute.org/whatsnew/2004G2GCompleteSurvey.pdf (accessed June 2, 2008).

Scatton, Kristen M. "Volunteers Pull Bug for United Way." *Republican & Herald* (Pottsville, Pennsylvania), November 2, 2007.

Schroeder, Charles C. "Meeting the Changing Needs of Students." In *Involvement in Campus Activities and the Retention of First-Year College Students,* edited by Tracy L. Skipper and Roxanne Argo, 19–34.

"Service-Learning is...," National Service-Learning Clearinghouse, n.d., http://www.service learning.org/welcome_to_service-learning/service-learning_is/index.php (accessed June 2, 2008).

Skipper, Tracy L., and Roxanne Argo, eds. *Involvement in Campus Activities and the Retention of First-Year College Students.* Columbia, SC: University of South Carolina, National Resource Center for The First-Year Experience and Students in Transition, 2003.

Smyth, Elaine B., and Robert S. Martin. "Working with Friends of the Library to Augment Staff Resources: A Case History." *Rare Books & Manuscripts Librarianship* 9, no. 1 (1994): 19–28.

Spring, Kimberly, Nathan Dietz, and Robert Grimm, Jr. *Educating for Active Citizenship: Service-Learning, School-Based Service and Youth Civic Engagement,* Youth Helping America series, Brief 2. Washington, DC: Corporation for National and Community Service, March 2006. http://www.nationalservice.gov/pdf/06_0323_SL_briefing.pdf (accessed June 2, 2008).

"Standards of Quality for School-Based and Community-Based Service Learning." Alliance for Service-Learning in Education Reform, March 1995. http://www.servicelearning.org/file manager/download/12/asler95.pdf (accessed June 2, 2008).

Bibliography

Straw, John B. "Friends Make a Difference." *Indiana Libraries* 25, no. 3 (2006): 13–15.

Sutton, Lynn, and H. David Womack. "Got Game? Hosting Game Night in an Academic Library." *College & Research Libraries News* 67, no. 3 (March 2006): 173–176.

Taylor, Merrily E. "It's Hard to Make New Friends: What to Think About in Creating a Friends of the Library Group." *Library Trends* 48, no. 3 (Winter 2000): 597–605.

Torney-Purta, Judith. "The School's Role in Developing Civic Engagement: A Study of Adolescents in Twenty-Eight Countries." *Applied Developmental Science* 6, no. 4 (2002): 203–212.

U.S. Dept. of Labor, Bureau of Labor Statistics, "Volunteering in the United States, 2006," (Jan. 10, 2007), USDL 07–0019, http://www.impactgiveback.org/PDF/VolunteeringUnitedStates2006.pdf (accessed June 2, 2008).

Ward, Deborah, ed. *Writing Grant Proposals That Win*. Sudbury, MA: Jones & Bartlett, 2006.

West, Edie. *The Big Book of Icebreakers: 50 Quick, Fun Activities for Energizing Meetings and Workshops*. New York: McGraw-Hill, 1999.

Woodward, Jeannette. *Creating the Customer-Driven Library: Building on the Bookstore Model*. Chicago: American Library Association, 2005.

Yates, Miranda, and James Youniss. "A Developmental Perspective on Community Service in Adolescence." *Social Development* 5, no 1 (March 1996): 85–111.

Yukl, Gary A. *Leadership in Organizations*. Upper Saddle River, NJ: Pearson/Prentice Hall, 2006.

Index

*Numbers in **bold italics** indicate pages with photographs*

Index

Index